UNJUSTIFIABLE
MEANS

UNJUSTIFIABLE MEANS

The Inside Story of How the CIA, Pentagon, and US Government Conspired to Torture

MARK FALLON

Regan Arts.

NEW YORK

Regan Arts.

New York, NY

First Regan Arts hardcover edition, October 2017

Library of Congress Control Number: 2016939709

ISBN 978-1-942872-79-5

Interior design by Nancy Singer
Cover design by Mike McQuade

Printed in the United States of America

10 9 8 7 6 5 4 3 2 1

This book is dedicated to Candace Jade Fallon,
our granddaughter, who was born into an uncertain world
and has brought so much joy and love into our lives.

CONTENTS

Should any American soldier be so base and infamous as to injure any [prisoner] . . . I do most earnestly enjoin you to bring him to such severe and exemplary punishment as the enormity of the crime may require. Should it extend to death itself, it will not be disproportional to its guilt as such a time and in such a cause . . . for by such conduct they bring shame, disgrace and ruin to themselves and their country.

—George Washington, September 1775, in orders issued to the northern expeditionary force of the Continental Army, under the command of Gen. Benedict Arnold

INTRODUCTION:
A NEW WARFARE

On September 11, 2001, the purposes and methods of war radically changed. A group of unsophisticated thugs, in service to a charismatic leader living in a distant cave, used a few thousand dollars to mount a surprise attack. Armed with seats purchased on airplanes, some rudimentary knowledge of flying, and box cutters, they executed one of the most successful military strikes in the history of the world, obliterating two of the world's largest buildings in the heart of the international financial industry and nearly scoring a direct hit on the Pentagon, America's supreme military command.

The world's most powerful country was momentarily helpless. Despite spending, in 2001, almost 22 percent of the annual federal budget—approximately $400 billion—to pay for the most highly trained military and the most sophisticated weapons ever known, the United States was revealed briefly as weak and confused. As so often happens at these crisis points, America had been looking in the wrong direction, back at what war had so long been rather than forward to what war was already becoming.

Whatever else it accomplished, 9/11 made crystal clear what the new rules of war would be: Soldiers wouldn't wear uniforms, nor would they represent a nation. They wouldn't attack a military target to control territory. They would slaughter civilians to control minds, and unlike most soldiers since the beginning of time, they didn't fear death. This was a secret army that needed no central command, only a loose recruiting and training structure based on destroying anything Amero-European in style, humanistic democracies, and their contagion of "anti-Islamic" modernity. To Americans and to our allies, the attacks of 9/11 seemed "irrational," "mindless," a "blind lashing out against Western culture." They were not. They reflected a calculated strategy that has yielded exactly the results the planners hoped for.

But the story is more nuanced than that. Al Qaeda, which quickly claimed responsibility for the attacks, didn't hate us for *who* we were so much as they hated us for *where* we were. The group had its roots in the ten-year Soviet occupation of Afghanistan that ended in 1989. Formed mostly of young Arab militants who flocked to Afghanistan to join the "holy war" against the Soviets, Al Qaeda's interests initially aligned with the US, and indeed (along with other Islamist extremists fighting the Russians), Al Qaeda received America financing and weaponry, along with training. But once the Soviets were driven out, Osama bin Laden, the wealthy young Arab who had become Al Qaeda's leader, turned his attention to the superpower that still retained a dominant position in the Muslim world: America.

Al Qaeda's aim was (and remains today, six years after bin Laden's death) to drive us—our institutions, our propaganda, our profit-making machinery, our religious colonizers—from the Middle East, just as they had driven the Soviet Union and its influences out of Afghanistan and elsewhere: a slow death, by a thousand cuts.

Al Qaeda sought a war of attrition in which they would provoke action that would attract more followers to their cause while slowly bleeding us of treasure, lives, and resolve.

While we focused on tactics, the adversary focused on strategies. As our death count grew, so did their number of followers, fed by many who had earlier immigrated to the West; by religious converts; and by once-moderates who now feared for their lives, families, and culture. Simply put, America got outplayed.

Even worse than that, America got changed. While brave men and women from all the military branches and across the entire range of intelligence services were putting their lives on the line in Iraq and Afghanistan (and in other places we will never know about) a darker strain of America emerged at Guantanamo Bay, Abu Ghraib, and too many other stark prisons and dank interrogation rooms. Under the pressure of a new kind of warfare, we threw away our vaunted democratic principles and turned our backs on international conventions the United States had proudly led the way in crafting. In the pursuit of "intelligence" coups that were never there to be scored in the first place, we employed interrogation methods borrowed from the Nazis and North Korean POW camps of a half-century earlier. We treated detainees as somehow subhuman, and in the process we became something less than human ourselves. Worst of all, we did all this under Washington's watchful eye and with its tacit and sometimes explicit encouragement.

This book is one man's perspective on the terror war, but it's a perspective rich with experience and often hard-won knowledge. I spent more than thirty years in counterintelligence and federal law enforcement—as a special agent for the Naval Criminal Investigative Service (NCIS) and as assistant director for training at the Federal Law Enforcement Training Centers within the Department of Homeland Security. As an NCIS special agent, I was involved in the prosecution of the Blind Sheik, Omar Abdel Rahman, the mastermind behind the 1993 bombing at the World Trade Center. In that same capacity I served as commander of the task force that investigated the lethal October 2000 attack on the USS *Cole* as it was being refueled in Yemen. I was also at the US naval base at Guantanamo Bay—Gitmo, as it became known—in the early days after 9/11, when there was still hope we would fight this battle consistent with American principles. And I was a frequent visitor at Gitmo only a few years later, when all hope of doing the war on terror right was already lost.

Bottom line: I've been on the front lines of the terror war every step of the way and for as long as almost anyone else can claim. I've seen what happens to conventional soldiers, case officers, and special agents alike, to their commanders, and to their political leaders when they must fight an enemy they don't understand, an enemy that instead of respecting their power and wealth sees both as evidence of their absolute corruption.

America then and still today is fighting an enemy that doesn't need a quick win because of budgets or election schedules. This is an enemy that is prepared to fight for centuries if necessary. Thanks to superior strategy in the new warfare, this enemy now controls a battlefield that is not a geographical location but a psychological terrain—a battlefield that promises to expose the truth about who we really are. It's the Battlefield of Terror.

What do terrorists want? To terrify, obviously. That's definitional. But terror is a long-term strategy in pursuit of a specific objective: to coerce reactive behavior. The real purpose is to instill enough fear that the enemy reacts irrationally. The strategic advantage happens over time. As the enemy cedes faith in its power and institutions to combat terror, it loses unifying purpose and atomizes into selfish interests. Stalin, Hitler, Pol Pot, and countless third-world tyrants used terror from the top down to make those they ruled fear and blame one another. These terrified masses invested their belief in the only power that could protect them: an autocratic government that was constantly inventing enemies, within and without. The new jihadists use terror from the bottom up with the same destabilizing purpose: to convince people to throw away their democratic visions of equality and the rule of law, replacing these virtues with brutal tribalism.

That's the lesson we should have kept in mind in the months after 9/11, and it's a lesson we forget at our own great peril today. Watching presidential candidates pledge allegiance to waterboarding and other discredited interrogation techniques during the 2016 primary campaign, I kept thinking ISIS, Al Qaeda, and our other enemies in the terror war don't need to seize a single piece of real estate to declare victory. If their brutality makes us brutal in turn, they win.

I wrote *Unjustifiable Means* because I felt compelled to. The torturers and their apologists have made a concerted effort to re-write history and shape the perception of the American public with dubious claims of heroic actions, but there's nothing heroic about abusing a defenseless human being. Those who committed such acts will have to live with the shame of what they did and the knowledge that their actions undoubtedly cost lives.

I was on the inside, in the arena, engaged in an almost daily battle to fulfill my orders not only to bring terrorists to justice but also to treat detainees humanely. I had a duty and did my job, and in the end I couldn't stop what I could see so clearly happening around me. That's my failure. But I tried. I spoke truth to power to protect the human rights of every detainee I was charged with investigating and bringing to justice. Of that, at least, I'm proud.

This book is my story, but it is also America's story—a story that needs to be told so we don't make the same mistakes again.

CHAPTER 1

"A MEAN, NASTY, DANGEROUS, DIRTY BUSINESS"

On the morning of October 12, 2000, a small motorboat approached the port side of the USS *Cole*, a guided missile destroyer anchored at a fueling island just offshore the harbor in Yemen's perpetually sunny city of Aden. As it pulled up alongside, the pilot detonated more than 500 pounds of explosives, tearing a huge hole in the side of the ship. The explosive force pushed up the floor of the galley above, killing crew members lining up for lunch. In the end, seventeen Americans died, along with the two suicide bombers. Al Qaeda, the then-ascendant terrorist group, claimed responsibility.

The US Navy responded by pulling all its ships out to sea. As the NCIS chief of counterintelligence operations for the Middle East, I became the tactical commander of the USS *Cole* task force. I was charged with leading the investigation into the bombing and collecting the intelligence to prevent a second or third or fourth attack elsewhere. Because NCIS serves as the navy and marine corps's FBI and CIA, we had to both find and prosecute those involved in the plot as well as do the intel work of clearing ports around the world so ships could come back in to dock. The assignment brought me deep inside the world of Al Qaeda.

One year later, minus a month and a day, Al Qaeda struck again. I was in London to brief senior European command and NATO authorities on "lessons learned" from the investigation of the USS *Cole* attack. In a nutshell, my conclusion was that it was preventable. More important by far, though, was the methodology we had developed for conducting investigations while pursuing members of Al Qaeda around the world. In the movies, bad guys don't crack until their interrogators have them begging for mercy, but in the real world, I had seen time and again that building rapport with detainees yielded far better actionable intelligence than the strong-arm approach, and prevented more attacks in the future. But by the time I was meant to share this information with some of the most brilliant and powerful military officers on the planet, the *Cole* investigation seemed like ancient news.

I was halfway through unpacking my clothes in my hotel room when I thought to turn on the TV and was suddenly confronted with the horrifying footage that is so well-known today: two commercial airliners slicing into the World Trade Center towers.

All of us have our own individual memories of 9/11. Mine is maybe unique—and definitely critical to this story. I thought of the Blind Sheik, the Egyptian cleric who orchestrated the 1993 bombing of the World Trade Center. Back in 1992, we had the Blind Sheik and his followers ready to walk into a trap, but the FBI had it called off, frightened of possible blowback. A year later, the FBI nabbed Ramzi Yousef after the World Trade Center bombing, but only after he had carried out the plot the Blind Sheik had sanctioned. While Yousef was being transported by helicopter past the World Trade Center, one of his FBI captors lifted his blindfold and pointed to the towers, taunting: "Look down there. They're still standing."

Yousef glanced over at the towers, then spat out, "They wouldn't be if I had enough money and explosives."

Turned out you didn't need that much money. Or even traditional explosives. Nineteen terrorists had gotten four commercial airliners to do the job for them.

Back in Washington, it was all hands on deck for the counterintelligence community, but President Bush had grounded air travel to the States, and that included me. Helplessly stuck in England that Sunday afternoon, I turned on the television in the London NCIS office, just in time to catch Dick Cheney describing his own 9/11 moments to Tim Russert on a special edition of *Meet the Press* broadcast from Camp David.

"A little before 9:00, my speechwriter came in," Cheney recalled. "We were going to go over some speeches coming up. And my secretary called in just as we were starting to meet just before 9:00 and said an airplane had hit the World Trade Center. That was the first one that went in. So we turned on the television and watched for a few minutes and then actually saw the second plane hit the World Trade Center. And as soon as that second plane showed up, that's what triggered the thought: *terrorism*."

Within minutes, the vice president had gathered national security adviser Condoleezza Rice, Cheney chief of staff Scooter Libby, and others, and patched through a call to George W. Bush in Florida. The group had just turned back to the TV when Cheney's Secret Service agents came bursting into the room.

"Under these circumstances, they just move," he told Russert. "They don't . . . ask politely. They came in and said, 'Sir, we have to leave immediately,' and grabbed me. . . . They're bigger than I am, and they hoisted me up and moved me very rapidly down the hallway, down some stairs, through some doors, and down some more stairs into an underground facility under the White House. And it's a, matter of fact, a corridor, locked at both ends. And they did that because they had received a report that an airplane was headed for the White House. . . . And when it entered the danger zone, it looked like it was headed for the White House; [that] was when they grabbed me and evacuated me to the basement."

Russert asked mostly the right questions. Cheney, in his unique, clench-jawed way, gave mostly the right answers. The vice president projected strength in the face of tragedy, control in the face of what was still a chaotic situation. I particularly liked the tail end of his response to a question about whether America and, by extension, the Bush administration had been adequately prepared for this attack or should have been more vigilant: "We're an open society," Cheney said. "We love it that way. It's very important to preserve that and not to let the terrorists win by turning ourselves into some kind of police state."

One part of the Cheney-Russert exchange, though, wouldn't leave me alone in the weeks that followed, in the same way the Blind Sheik kept breaking into my dreams at night. Tim Russert's question could not possibly have taken the vice president by surprise. It was a Journalism 101 query: "There have been restrictions placed on the United States' intelligence gathering, a reluctance to use unsavory characters, those who violate human rights, to assist in intelligence gathering. Will we lift some of those restrictions?"

Cheney's answer, whether it was rehearsed or not, appeared intent on sending a message at multiple levels: to our enemies, our allies, our nation and, more intimately, to people like me. "Well, I think so," he told Russert, starting calmly. "I think one of the by-products, if you will, of this tragic set of circumstances is that we'll see a very thorough sort of reassessment of how we operate and the kinds of people we deal with. If you want to deal only with sort of officially approved, certified good guys, you're not going to find out what the bad guys are doing. You need to be able to penetrate these organizations. You need to have on the payroll some very unsavory characters if, in fact, you're going to be able to learn all that needs to be learned in order to forestall these kinds of activities.

"It is a mean, nasty, dangerous, dirty business out there, and we have to operate in that arena. I'm convinced we can do it. We can do it successfully. But we need to make certain that we have not tied the hands, if you will, of our intelligence communities in terms of accomplishing their mission."

Uh-oh, I thought. *Untying those hands would be a fucking disaster.* Little did I know how much of one.

CHAPTER 2

MIND GAMES

The federal government had a frantic air about it in the weeks and months just after 9/11. Just getting back to the States from London had been an odyssey: Heathrow to Italy, Italy to Spain, then to the Azores. I finally landed at Langley Air Force Base in Norfolk, Virginia, at three in the morning on September 20, and three hours later was on a commercial flight to Tampa International Airport. When we arrived, the airport looked nothing like the ones I was used to. Virtually everyone was in a uniform of some sort. The place looked more like a military base in a combat zone than a commercial airport in America.

From Tampa International I went to MacDill Air Force Base, which was even more on edge. The base is the nerve center for Central Command (CENTCOM), which oversees a huge swath of US military operations in a part of the world that suddenly had infested national nightmares. CENTCOM's area of responsibility stretches from Egypt to Afghanistan, including Iran, Iraq, Jordan,

Lebanon, Pakistan, Qatar, Saudi Arabia, Syria, Tajikistan, Turkmenistan, United Arab Emirates, Uzbekistan, and Yemen—a who's who of terrorist enclaves. Special Operations Command (SOCOM), located just down the street on the base, exercises command and control over all US Special Operations forces worldwide, everything from Green Berets to Navy SEALs—the very people likely to be most active in the opening stages of whatever retribution was to follow.

My new mission, and pretty much the hard focus of everyone at MacDill, was to find the terrorists, locate their money, ID their friends, figure out what they were planning, and make sure that plan didn't happen. I didn't yet know what exact position I would end up with in this new war paradigm, but I knew it would involve criminal investigations, counterintelligence operations, and interrogations with an eye to bringing the bad guys to trial, and in the months ahead I worked as hard as I could to get ready for whatever came my way.

In the world I traveled in, urgency was the rule, not the exception. Something awful and unparalleled in American history had happened. If you weren't in near-constant motion, you felt like a slacker, almost unpatriotic. In a way, I might have felt it more than most. While I had been checking into my comfortable London hotel on 9/11, my colleagues in the home office—at the Washington Navy Yard, about a mile and a half from the US Capitol and maybe twice that distance from the White House—had been picking up word that yet another terrorist-controlled airliner was heading toward their own backyard. Dick Cheney had been hustled off to a bunker-like corridor. My friends, like a lot of DC federal workers, scrambled wherever they could.

And we all continued to scramble in one way or another for months to follow. Once Al Qaeda claimed responsibility for 9/11—

and that took less than four days—there was never any question about sending Special Ops forces into Afghanistan to hunt for bin Laden. Could Iraq be far behind? That war drum was beating too, long before the US-led coalition had invaded Iraq on March 20, 2003.

What I didn't realize in this flurry of activity was that all our efforts to track, interrogate, and prosecute the bad guys were being radically undermined by a collaboration of distinguished academics and high-ranking government officials.

At a December 15–16, 2001, gathering far from MacDill—at a lavish home in Wynnewood, a patrician, close-in western suburb of Philadelphia—a group of well-regarded academics and government officials was preparing to fight fire with fire.

Attendees at the meeting included distinguished professors from the University of Washington, Wesleyan, Duke, Penn, the University of North Carolina, and elsewhere. Foreign academics were present too: Ariel Merari, director of the Political Violence Research Unit at Tel Aviv University in Israel; S. J. Rachman, an emeritus psychology professor at the University of British Columbia in Vancouver; and Emmanuel Sivan, professor of Islamic studies at Hebrew University of Jerusalem. Government attendees included ███████████████ the FBI's Behavioral Science Unit; ███████████████ the FBI's Behavioral Analysis Unit East; ████████████████████████████ ████████████████████████ and James Mitchell, a CIA contract psychologist.

The central figure of the gathering was Martin Seligman, the Robert A. Fox Leadership Professor of Psychology at the University of Pennsylvania. Although the meeting had been convened largely at the request of the CIA's ███████████, Seligman was its host and star attraction. The meeting was held at his house, a sprawling mansion that had once belonged to the great maestro Eugene Ormandy and now—according to *Philadelphia* magazine—featured a near-life-size portrait of Seligman himself over the mantelpiece.

Seligman could afford such luxuries. A former president of the American Psychological Association, he was generally credited with being the father of the highly popular field of Positive Psychology. He had already written best sellers on the subject, and would go on to write many more. Seligman's website is rich with quotes on the subject, drawn from his 2002 mega–best seller *Authentic Happiness.* Many reflect the simple and optimistic style that has made him so popular: "Use your signature strengths and virtues in the service of something much larger than you are" and, "[Positive Psychology] takes you through the countryside of pleasure and gratification, up into the high country of strength and virtue, and finally to the peaks of lasting fulfillment: meaning and purpose." Seligman had even crusaded on the subject to his own profession, using his 1998 inauguration as APA president to urge his colleagues to study what makes happy people happy.

His audience at the December 2001 meeting, though, hadn't come to hear the host spout bromides about happiness. Their interest was in an earlier book, Seligman's 1975 study titled "Helplessness: On Depression, Development, and Death." While conducting psychological research on canines earlier in his career, Seligman had discovered that when dogs were indiscriminately given electric shocks they couldn't avoid, they would fail to take action to prevent subsequent shocks even when an escape route was readily available. In effect, they "learned" helplessness.

To Seligman, this insight came with a huge upside. If people, like dogs, could learn helplessness, then they also could learn optimism as a pathway out of depression. (Thus, with many in-between steps, was born Positive Psychology.) Seligman's audience, however, was interested in taking his research in the opposite direction: not as a pathway to positivism but as an entry point into a world where prisoners would have learned helplessness so well they would be unable to resist telling interrogators their darkest secrets.

In fact, Marty Seligman's learned helplessness research married well with an older, deeper strain in the psychology of torture. Back in 1957, an air force social scientist named Albert D. Biderman had authored a study titled "Communist Attempts to Elicit False Confessions from Air Force Prisoners of War." Based on interviews with air force personnel who had been held in North Korean POW camps, Biderman's paper contained a chart of the types of physical and psychological conditions the North Koreans and their Chinese Communist mentors had created and imposed to weaken their captives' ability to resist complying with the will of their abusers.

The study centered on how, through the manipulation of a prisoners' environment and perceptions, both physical and mental, jailers could brainwash them. The North Korean prison-camp interrogators used isolation to deprive captives of social support and create a dependency on the interrogators for emotional support. The immediate predicament of the prisoners was totally under the control of their captors. The captors insisted on total compliance even for food, clothing, or social contact. In addition to isolation, total darkness (or, alternatively, constant bright lights), and restriction of movement were used to foster total helplessness. Biderman's paper also described how American prisoners were tortured by making them stand "for exceedingly long periods" in "extremely cold" conditions.

The study's accompanying "coercion chart" puts a finer point on the conditions prisoners were exposed to. The chart includes using humiliation and degradation to induce both mental and physical exhaustion and thus weaken the ability and will to resist complying with the abusers' wishes. No question, the North Koreans—and their Chinese Communist instructors—were very successful at leveraging psychological torture to control their detainees and attain confessions. There was only one problem with this interrogation process: the confessions were all false. Psychologically breaking prisoners made them repeat whatever their interrogators wanted. In its purest form, breaking prisoners as Biderman described even made the prisoners believe what they said, but it was hardly a truth serum.[*]

Albert Biderman, it should be noted, considered such

---

[*] To quote from Biderman's article, "Communist Methods":

The kind of "confession" we are discussing consists of considerably more than the signing of a piece of paper, which says: "On such and such a date I committed such and such a crime—signed John Jones." It consists of considerably more than making an equivalent oral statement in a court. These "confession"-extortion efforts involved the attempt to manipulate the individual so that he behaves over an extended period as if:

he actually committed certain concrete acts which he can "describe" with meticulous detail;

these acts were "criminal," in the sense of being violations of the most fundamental standards of human decency;

these acts were not isolated transgressions but manifestation of a "criminal" pattern in his thought and action;

his "crimes" were part and parcel of a larger nefarious political conspiracy;

his "criminal" role was motivated by a self-seeking alignment with this political conspiracy, of which he was only a pawn;

he is now remorseful and repentant;

his changed attitude is due to new-found political conviction for which he is indebted to his patient captors.

In this extreme form of "confession"-elicitation, as encountered by our men, the objective was not merely having the prisoner "confirm" that certain acts were committed, but rather to have his behavior confirm the entire world-view of the Communists relevant to those acts. (*From the Bulletin of the New York Academy of Medicine, Vol. 33, No. 9, September 1957.*)

techniques, "abominable outrages. . . . Probably no other aspect of Communism reveals more thoroughly its disrespect for truth and individuals than its resort to these techniques." But the CIA had historically kept a more open mind on the kind of practices Biderman described, and their ultimate efficacy in yielding actionable intelligence.

Ever since its founding in the wake of World War II, the CIA had been looking for consistent results in prying loose secrets from America's enemies. Experiments included giving massive doses of LSD to unsuspecting bar patrons, while agents observed behind a one-way mirror (a suicide ended that program), as well as sensory overload and sensory deprivation techniques. In 1963 the Agency even published a secret manual titled *KUBARK Counterintelligence Interrogation*, which borrowed directly from the interrogation techniques Biderman had compiled. The ultimate goal, according to the manual, was "establishing a sense of omnipotence . . . and omniscience of the captor."

True, the CIA had never achieved the success in such endeavors that it credited to the North Koreans, or the Chinese or Soviets or Germans before them. The Gestapo's Verschärfte Vernehmung, or "sharpened interrogation" program, had a particular allure because of its heavy reliance on the "scientific method." Not only were prisoners beaten and subjected to severe cold and other rigors, but technicians methodically recorded the results in the pursuit of perfecting methods. But maybe an American scientific discovery, "learned helplessness," would be the pathway drug all the Agency interrogators dreamed of.

Ostensibly, the meeting at Martin Seligman's Wynnewood mansion was of a group called Academics on Patrol and was held to discuss the subject of "How to Win the Peace" in the wake of all that had been happening in the three months since 9/11. No transcript of the proceedings has ever emerged publicly, if indeed a transcript or recording was made, but Seligman did produce a summary document shortly after the meeting that contained "six policy recommendations* aimed at winning a victory that will lastingly contain global terrorism." None of the six recommendations dealt even indirectly with using "learned helplessness" to break the will of captives, and Seligman has said publicly many times that the subject of torture was never raised at the meeting.

Seligman has made the same assertion about a three-hour talk he gave four months later, in April 2002, at the navy's SERE school in San Diego. SERE, pronounced "sear," is an acronym for Survival, Evasion, Resistance, and Escape. The training was developed to help Special Forces and other military avoid being captured. Much of the training is similar to the pumped-up outdoorsmen skills Sylvester Stallone's John Rambo used in *First Blood*: wilderness survival, building fires, navigating, emergency first aid, camouflage, and so on, but there's also a segment about how to survive if you are caught, including resistance to interrogation. For verisimilitude, personnel who take SERE training are tortured to get a taste of what kind of treatment they might be subject to if captured by an enemy so brutal it doesn't observe the Geneva Conventions on such matters.

---

* An independent review headed by David H. Hoffman wrote in the *Report to the Special Committee of the Board of Directors of the AMA*: "At the close of the meeting, the group had made 'six policy recommendations aimed at winning a victory that will lastingly contain global terrorism': Isolate Jihad Islam from Moderate Islam worldwide; [n]eutralize Saudi support for jihad Islamic fundamentalism worldwide; [p] olice the Arab Diaspora in Western Europe forcefully; [s]ubvert the social structure of terrorist organizations; [b]reak the link between the terrorists and the pyramid of sympathizers; [and] [b]uild American knowledge of Arab and Muslim culture and language."

Whatever Seligman's intent, the inescapable facts are: A) his concept of learned helplessness became central to interrogation techniques used in the years just after 9/11, B) those techniques at the very least would freely violate the Geneva Conventions on torture, and C) the biggest evangelists for learned helplessness were in many cases alumni of either the Wynnewood meeting, Seligman's SERE school talk, or—in the case of James Mitchell—both.

A psychologist well schooled in SERE resistance principles, Jim Mitchell had retired from the US Air Force the previous May and was working as a private contractor to the CIA at the time of the Wynnewood gathering. So inspired was Mitchell by Seligman's presentation on learned helplessness that he almost immediately began collaborating with his friend, John "Bruce" Jessen, chief of psychology services for the Joint Personnel Recovery Agency (JPRA), which oversaw the SERE program.

With astonishing speed, Mitchell and Jessen coauthored two February 2002 documents. The first, "Recognizing and Developing Countermeasures to Al-Qa'ida Resistance to Interrogation Techniques: A Resistance Training Perspective," drew heavily on established SERE protocols. The second, a military memo circulated by Jessen, took the next step. Titled "Prisoner Handling Recommendations," it incorporated what both men had quickly absorbed about learned helplessness and what they already knew about SERE, and advanced specific interrogation protocols. (The memo remains classified today, a decade and a half after it was circulated to those with proper clearance.)

Among the doctors' recommendations: shoving detainees into a wall, grabbing and slapping them, placing them in cramped and dark confinement boxes with or without insects to exploit any potential phobias (David Lean's 1957 film *The Bridge on the River Kwai* comes to mind, for those old enough to remember it), prolonged standing, stress positions, sleep deprivation, and waterboarding to produce the sensation of drowning and suffocation—i.e., torture.

As subsequent investigations would show, neither Mitchell nor Jessen had any legitimate interrogation experience. Mitchell's SERE training involved resisting illegal interrogation tactics, not conducting successful legal ones. And neither had more than a superficial understanding of the Middle East or Al Qaeda. What they did have, though, was an eerie sense of timing, and in the post-9/11 chaos, that was enough to make both of them rich.

Almost immediately after the joint-authored documents, Jessen retired from the military, joined the private sector, and began doing contract work, with Mitchell, for the CIA. Eventually, the two psychologists formed a company they called Mitchell Jessen & Associates. The "associates" came to include two prominent ex-CIA officials. The first, ██████████, had helped arrange the December 2001 meeting at Seligman's house and had held a high-ranking position at the CIA's Research and Analysis Branch. The second was psychologist ████████, who quit the CIA to join Mitchell and Jessen. After leaving, she maintained close contacts at the highest levels of the CIA, including one of the agency's senior lawyers—and her husband ████████████.

A rising tide lifts all ships, and a $181 million consulting contract with the CIA assured everyone at Mitchell Jessen & Associates would be floating high. Yet another beneficiary of Mitchell and Jessen's great success was Joseph Matarazzo, an Oregon psychologist who, like Seligman, had previously served as president of the American Psychological Association. Matarazzo owned 1 percent of Mitchell and Jessen's company. Then in his late eighties, Matarazzo was still consulting occasionally on professional issues and delivered an opinion that sleep deprivation—one of the interrogation methods Mitchell and Jessen were promoting—did not necessarily amount to torture.

Mitchell and Jessen hadn't invented anything new. They simply took the interrogation practices Albert Biderman had charted in the mid-1950s, married them with what Martin Seligman had uncovered while randomly shocking dogs in the 1970s, and called the hybrid enhanced interrogation techniques—EITs for short. The "enhanced" part of that was learned helplessness. Together, the two psychologists and their all-star ex-CIA team took EITs on the road, seeking converts to the theory that learned helplessness created a baseline condition that would ultimately result in the acquisition of accurate and reliable information.

I didn't find out about the actual meeting at Marty Seligman's house until years later, but I was embedded deeply enough in the counterterrorism community that I began picking up vibes even before Mitchell and Jessen published their February 2002 paper about learned helplessness and how experiments that had involved torturing dogs were somehow going to usher in a whole new era of hyper-effective interrogation. I remember worrying at the time that any interrogation approach that stressed harsh methods might play to the emotional strain that so many of us had been under since 9/11. Revenge in one form or another was on nearly everyone's mind. I also remember thinking that, like so many other counterintelligence fads, this too would pass.

For starters, we had shown time and again at the NCIS that building a relationship with detainees ultimately yielded far more useful intelligence than slapping them around the interrogation room, or worse. The more you beat up on people, the harder they work to figure out what you want to hear. In essence, interrogators are instructing them on the truth they must admit to stop the pain—the false confessions that Albert Biderman studied so intently. Our approach went in the exact opposite direction: detainees end up telling their interrogators the truth because they have earned the right to know it. Judge for yourself which method is likely to produce a "truth" that is really true.

What's more, I was close to a top-notch CIA operational psychologist, ███████████████, who was a strong advocate of rapport-based interrogating and would be sure to resist any movement toward the sort of brutality learned helplessness implied, especially when practiced on human beings. And ███████ wasn't alone at the CIA in favoring our approach.

Even more important, teaching "helplessness" through electric shocks or sleep deprivation or beating people with sticks or however else the Nazis and North Koreans might have done it simply wasn't legal. The Geneva Conventions and the Eighth Amendment to the US Constitution forbid cruel and unusual punishment.

That's got to be firewall enough, I told myself.

CHAPTER 3

A PLAGUE OF LAWYERS

It's too simple to say the actual war on terror was waged by brave men and women risking everything while the war against terrorists was fought by psychologists and lawyers. But simple is not always wrong. Even before Marty Seligman's comments at Wynnewood inspired at least several of his fellow psychologists to dream big torture dreams, some of the government's top attorneys were hard at work assuring the war footing Dick Cheney sought and the intelligence-gathering tools Jim Mitchell, Bruce Jessen, and others would soon propose as most effective would meet as little legal resistance as possible.

In the last three months of 2001, everything seemed to be happening at once. The nation was recovering from a horrible shock. Bodies were still being removed from the rubble of the World Trade Center towers. Every news cycle added fresh details to our understanding of the hijackers, and Osama bin Laden and Al Qaeda behind them. US Special Forces were already operational in Afghanistan. The Bush administration was talking darkly of bio-logical weapons and weapons of mass destruction—WMDs as they became known—stockpiled in Iraq.

Yet for all the fervor that so colored events in the aftermath of 9/11, the series of legal decisions that would ultimately be used to justify torture unfolded more like an avalanche seen in extra-slow motion: a boulder comes loose at the top of the mountain and be-gins rolling downhill, leisurely picking up more rocks and stones and boulders as it goes along until the whole mass—which in slow motion looked so much like a geological ballet when it began—suddenly ends up crashing into the valley below in a deafening roar. That's where I was standing, in the valley at the bottom of the mountain, when the onslaught arrived. But that gets ahead of the story.

On September 18, 2001, exactly one week after the carnage in lower Manhattan, the Pentagon, and near Shanksville, Pennsylvania, President Bush signed Senate Joint Resolution 23, "Authorization for Use of Military Force." The resolution, Bush said in his signing statement, "recognizes the seriousness of the terrorist threat to our nation and the authority of the president under the constitution to take action to deter and prevent acts of terrorism against the United States. . . . Our whole nation is unalterably committed to a direct, forceful, and comprehensive response to these terrorist attacks and the scourge of terrorism directed against the United States and its interests."

All that's a matter of public record. As yet, though, there has been no release of the "Memorandum of Notification" the president signed a day earlier, authorizing the Central Intelligence Agency to capture ▮▮▮▮▮ interrogate Al Qaeda leaders. While the gist of the memorandum is public and portions have been released, the memorandum remains so secret that even the font it was typed in is still classified. The document became known as the Gloves Come Off memo. At roughly the same time, Bush signed off ███

██

██

None of that threatened the rule of law, but it cracked the door slightly, and a few weeks later, Roger Ailes, then the head of Fox News, gave it a further push. According to Bob Woodward's *Bush at War*, Ailes used Karl Rove as the go-between for a memo that implored the president to use "the harshest measures possible" in dealing with the terrorism network behind the September attacks. Otherwise, Ailes cautioned, the public would quickly lose patience with his administration.

Whatever the influence Ailes's memo might have had on the president's subsequent decision making—and Woodward thinks it was significant—on November 13, 2001, Bush signed a military order titled "Detention, Treatment, and Trial of Certain Non-Citizens in the War Against Terrorism."

Three items in particular near the end of the presidential "findings" began to define the new world I would soon be operating in: One, individuals "subject to the order" henceforth "were to be detained, and, when tried, to be tried for violations of the laws of war and other applicable laws by military tribunals." Two, given the situation, it was "not practicable to apply in military commissions under this order the principles of law and the rules of evidence generally recognized in the trial of criminal cases in the United States district courts." And three, given the probability of further terrorist attacks on the homeland, "an extraordinary emergency exists for national defense purposes."

In section 2 of the memorandum, "Definition and Policy," Bush and his lawyers further clarified who would be subject to this order: "any individual who is not a United States citizen" and whom the president has "reason to believe" might be a member of Al Qaeda and/or "has engaged in, aided or abetted, or conspired to commit, acts of international terrorism, threatened to cause, or have as their aim to cause injury to or averse effects on the United States, its citizens, national security, foreign policy, or economy; or has knowingly harbored one or more individuals" who have done any of the preceding.

Not only were rules of evidence being dispensed with in this "extraordinary emergency," the detention gates—and military tribunals—were being thrown wide open to anyone the president had "reason to believe" was a terrorist, threatened to do harm to America or Americans, or gave aid and comfort to same. That, I told myself, was potentially a very large gene pool. Given the sweeping vagueness of the "definition," it also could end up being just about any size the president and his people wanted it to be.

One other thing the November memorandum did: it effectively took the 9/11 investigation out of the hands of the FBI—the agency legally responsible for federal crimes, including terrorism—and placed it instead with DOD, the Department of Defense.

Was that a big surprise to me? Not really. Washington is a constant power-grab, especially in times of crisis. Donald Rumsfeld, then the defense secretary, had been playing that game for a long time, going back to the Nixon administration, while Bob Mueller had taken over at the FBI just seven days before 9/11. With power-grabbing, practice makes perfect. But I can't say I was happy with the change. The FBI has some of the best counterterrorism people I've ever worked with, and the USS *Cole* investigation had given me a front seat on maybe the finest counterterrorism investigation and interrogations I've ever been involved in.

One of the subjects in that interrogation was a Yemeni, Jamal

Badawi, suspected of helping run the logistics cell for the *Cole* attack. The interrogators were NCIS special agent Ken Reuwer and FBI agent ████████, an Arabic speaker who had grown up in the Middle East. Ken didn't speak Arabic, so ██ did most of the talking during the interrogation, but Ken would hear what the translator said and pass ██ notes. It was all respectful, all in keeping with prosecutorial requirements—Badawi was even read his Miranda rights. There was no strong-arming, no threats, nothing that might have come anywhere near appearing on Albert Biderman's torture chart or in one of Marty Seligman's introductory lectures on learned helplessness. Yet in the end Jamal Badawi rolled on everybody—an intelligence-collection bonanza. He not only admitted to his own role in the USS *Cole* attack cell; he also identified other Al Qaeda members and safe houses. Badawi even implicated Fahd al-Quso, who later emerged as the second-in-command of Al Qaeda in the Arabian Peninsula. As was the case with Badawi, ██████ and NCIS special agent Robert McFadden skillfully interrogated al-Quso. The results were the same: actionable intelligence and untainted evidence.

With the FBI down a rank or two in the pecking order, it was going to be harder to bring people like ████████ in on the action. But we had gone to school on all this at NCIS, and our duty was fundamentally unchanged by the decrees issued to date. We were a military resource. This was now a military command-and-control issue, with DOD at the top. George Bush had written in his November memorandum that he would base his prosecutorial decisions on "reasons to believe." Our job was to produce those reasons to believe for the president, with an eye to military tribunals, and all our efforts would be pointed in that direction. Then, just when our work was becoming clearer, something totally unexpected happened.

• • •

I was thrust into the middle of this emerging legal battlefield at 5:45 in the morning by the secure telephone at my home. It was Sunday, December 9, 2001. When that phone rings in the early morning or on weekends, it is never a good sign. This was no exception.

"Hello?"

"Mark? It's Jimmy. Sorry to get you out of bed on a Sunday, but there's been a development in Afghanistan." Jim MacFarlane was the number two at NCIS's Middle East Field Office.

"No problem. What's up, Jimmy?" I asked.

"The Northern Alliance found an American with a bunch of other Taliban POWs. He's gonna be taken to either Camp Rhino or the USS *Bataan*."

"Really?" I said. My mind was racing. An American fighting with the Taliban? What was he thinking? None of our planning included that possibility. This was going to change everything. "What's his name?"

"John Walker Lindh," said Jim. "Apparently he was fingered by one of the other prisoners as an English speaker. He initially told the CIA he was Irish."

"Well, that didn't work." I reached for the legal codebooks I kept next to the phone.

There were two laws regarding aiding the enemy: Article 104 of the UCMJ (Uniformed Code of Military Justice) and 10USC904 of the US Criminal Code. They both basically agreed. Under UCMJ, if Lindh had aided the Taliban or Al Qaeda with materials or passed them information, he was subject to court-martial. If guilty, he could be sentenced to a number of penalties, including execution. But whether Lindh ended up in a military or civilian court, he had the same basic rights. He got to see a lawyer and he didn't have to talk. Also, we couldn't just hold Lindh at Camp Rhino, in the far south of Afghanistan, indefinitely. That might work with Afghan detainees, but this guy was a bona fide American, whatever he had done. At some point down the road—and not too far—we would probably have to find a way to move him onto American soil. Where that might be was anyone's guess.

"Listen," I told Jimmy. "It doesn't matter whether this ends up being a criminal investigation or counterintelligence matter. We need to get agents there to talk to this guy."

"Agreed. We're on it," said Jimmy.

We planned to talk again soon. I walked over to my home office and closed the door quietly so as not to wake my wife.

I worked most of the day, only taking a break to eat and watch my Giants lose an ugly game at Dallas. I headed into the NCIS's Anti-Terrorist Alert Center (now the Multiple Threat Alert Center) at about 3:30 Monday morning. Lindh's capture had the place abuzz. Netting a young, white US citizen, born in Washington, DC, added a scary new dimension for a nation already on edge. Ever since 9/11, we'd ramped up additional screening at ports of entry into the United States, but Lindh didn't come anywhere near fitting the stereotypical profile of an Islamic terrorist.

Even if he was just a foot soldier for the Taliban or low-level Al Qaeda, Lindh's existence prompted critical questions: How was an upper-middle-class kid from suburban California recruited into militant Islam? What training had he received? What was his mission? How many other Westerners were there? Were there sleeper cells in the United States? We wanted to know who, what, when, where, how, and why. Of course, we weren't alone.

I called up Klain Garriga, the head of NCIS's office in the Middle East. Klain was a Vietnam vet who had come out of the war with a Silver Star and shrapnel still lodged in his body. I had met him decades ago at NCIS basic training, and we worked together on the streets in the Philippines.

Klain didn't waste time. "I've got a C-130 ready to leave within an hour," he said. The four-person team included an Arabic speaker, an interrogator, an operational psychologist, and a Judge Advocate General's Corps (JAGC) lawyer—all ready to fly to Camp Rhino and talk to Lindh.

"Does the JAGC think Lindh is subject to UCMJ [Uniform Code of Military Justice]?" I asked.

"Yeah, that's what he's telling me," said Klain.

"Yeah, that's what I read too."

The ongoing USS *Cole* investigation had given NCIS the most experience in the military with investigating Islamic terrorist networks. We were ready to go and find out what Lindh could tell us. If only it was that simple. Later that day I got word from another JAGC lawyer that we were not to interrogate Lindh: "Stand by for twenty-four hours." Hurry up and wait.

Lindh was a popular guy. When I talked with FBI headquarters, it was clear the Bureau was sore that the marines had custody of Lindh. I understood their position. The army also wanted its criminal investigation division to hold on to Lindh as a prisoner of war so that US Army Criminal Investigation Command (CID) could interrogate him. Problem was, while CID agents were good at processing crime scenes and routine criminal investigations on army posts, they lacked any counterintelligence training or experience. The uniqueness of these circumstances was simply beyond CID's capabilities.

Meanwhile the Department of Defense was talking to the Department of Justice, also trying to figure out who got first dibs on Lindh. Everyone was lining up to interview him at Camp Rhino, ourselves included. Over the rest of the week, I worked the phones but couldn't get clarity on just about anything. Richard Shiffrin, a top Department of Defense attorney for intelligence matters, was advising on Lindh for the Pentagon, and had been helpful at first, but the ground kept shifting beneath all of us. On Tuesday, for example, Shiffrin advised me that NCIS should conduct interviews in theater, probably Afghanistan. The next day, though, we were stood down; the army had refused to let us in. Meanwhile, more enemy prisoners of war were piling up at Camp Rhino, including another Westerner, a blond-haired Australian named David Hicks.

To cover all my bases, I was requesting a 31B form for interrogations—the military version of Miranda rights, such as remaining silent and having access to a lawyer. Even though I was a civilian, I was working for the military and had to go through its legal channels. But I still didn't know whether a rights waiver was required for our NCIS guys when we finally got to interview Lindh. The JAGC and US attorneys said yes. My contact at the Department of Defense, Shiffrin, had shifted his focus from criminal investigation to purely intelligence exploitation.

Then the Pentagon began parsing words about Lindh's interrogation being an intelligence interview versus a criminal interview. Instead of one interview to serve both ends, they started talking about separate interviews to avoid tainting any of the information that we might end up using on the criminal side. Translation: the tactics used during the intel interview would be harsher than what is allowed during a criminal interview.

Then, before any of our investigators got to Lindh, he was gone. On December 14, under the cover of darkness, Lindh, Hicks, and three other detainees were hustled on board a navy helicopter and flown to the USS *Peleliu* in the north Arabian Sea. There, the ship's masters-at-arms assumed custody of Lindh. The American Taliban, as he became known, was in navy hands now.

The transfer didn't stay a secret long. Four days later, a head-line in the *Washington Post* read 5 DETAINEES HELD ON US SHIP. The article gave the details of the fly-by-night transfer. The American Civil Liberties Union quickly filed a suit challenging both the constitutionality and necessity of a military commission process, as opposed to charging the prisoners in a criminal court. The media exposure of a secret shipboard detention program was not what anyone wanted. Agencies were ducking responsibility left and right.

In theory, having Lindh in navy hands should have served our purposes at NCIS—we were, after all, navy-based. But the ongoing high-level debate about who would have access to Lindh and for what purposes meant we were still unable to interview him for days. Intel groups from the United States Marine Corps, the Defense Intelligence Agency, and the FBI joined us in urgently requesting to interview Lindh and the other detainees. The Australians also wanted to talk to Hicks. But we were still stymied by a lack of clear policy or guidance. An American Taliban posed a unique challenge that hidebound bureaucrats simply could not respond to. Regulations were out the window. Precedent didn't exist. Suddenly, important policy decisions were being made ad hoc at the most senior levels, often by lawyers with no technical expertise. Even if John Walker Lindh was a minor foot soldier, or not even that, he had thrown the counterterrorism mechanism off kilter.

Equally alarming was the quick reemergence of a kind of "agency tribal" behavior. My USS *Cole* presentation that had been scheduled for September 11 focused on this phenomenon. The US has seven-teen separate intel agencies, many with overlapping responsibilities. Each developed its own culture—the FBI was not the CIA was not the NSA. Even within the armed forces, the NCIS had little in common with the army CID. Cooperation didn't come easily. I had friends in, and access to, the CIA, but I still had trouble convincing case officers that we weren't competitors. "Look," I'd say, "While you guys are working the champagne circuit ███████████, we're working the beer and whiskey circuit in the ports." Not that secrets didn't sometimes get served along with the hors d'oeuvres at black-tie events, but plenty of good intel came from the ports too.

I'd also seen military or legal missions undermined when the power or status of a particular tribe—be it an agency, branch of the service, or prosecutor's office in the legal system—took precedence over larger mission goals. Honestly, it was a big part of what stopped us from connecting the dots before 9/11. Now, three months later, just as we were gearing up for what should be a coordinated effort to interrogate detainees and begin moving them into the military justice system, it was happening again.

Just as alarming, I was getting hints that what constituted acceptable interrogation practices might be open to question. One friend told me that Richard Shiffrin, the Defense Department lawyer I was working with to get directives on Lindh, had called up the JPRA, the agency responsible for SERE training. This was right at the start of 2002. Mitchell and Jessen's papers advocating learned helplessness hadn't yet been published, but like me, Shiffrin had picked up word that the CIA was exploring new "scientific" measures to overcome Al Qaeda resistance to interrogation and that these measures somehow dovetailed with SERE "exploitation tactics."

I don't know if the call to the JPRA was at Shiffrin's own initiative or if he was directed to call. As far as I know, no one at the JPRA told him the measures entailed torture tactics, not interrogation techniques, but perhaps that should have been obvious.

The first consensus that developed around Lindh was an agreement not to refer to him as a "captive" or "prisoner of war" but rather as an "unlawful belligerent." The word choice was not just semantic.

Prisoners of war have clear judicial rights under the Geneva Conventions and federal law. Unlawful belligerents do not. The different labels created a whole new category of person with practically no existing applicable precedent or legislation to protect them. That allowed government lawyers a lot more latitude in dealing with, for example, the ACLU lawsuit over secret shipboard detention.

About a week after Lindh and the four others were transferred to the *Peleliu*, we finally got clarity on the ground rules for interrogation. Our NCIS investigators were going to be allowed to use an interview room in the ship's rear brig. They were first instructed not to issue Lindh any warnings about his rights. The interview would be purely for intel exploitation. I wasn't thrilled by the conditions, but at least we were going to be able to talk to a potentially valuable source.

Then the lawyers struck again. On December 27, 2001, Secretary of Defense Donald Rumsfeld announced that prisoners from Afghanistan would be transferred to the naval base at Guantanamo Bay, or GTMO (pronounced Gitmo) in military abbreviation. The next day, Deputy Assistant Attorneys General Patrick Philbin and John Yoo sent a memorandum to William "Jim" Haynes, the general counsel at the Department of Defense that gave a bit more insight into why they were considering Guantanamo.

Technically the land that naval base sits on still belongs to Cuba; the US is just leasing it in perpetuity. This gave a beachhead for Department of Justice lawyers to argue that Guantanamo isn't actually in US sovereign territory. The Philbin/Yoo memorandum, titled "Possible Habeas Jurisdiction over Aliens Held in Guantanamo Bay, Cuba," claimed federal courts had no jurisdiction there and could not review Guantanamo detainee mistreatment or mistaken arrest cases. It also stated that international laws did not apply in the "war on terror." Detainees held there would exist in a sort of legal twilight, neither prisoner of war captured on a traditional battlefield nor inmate held on American territory.

Three weeks later, President Bush ███████████████ seemed to grow organically from Philbin and Yoo's memorandum. This one stated that ███████████████

███████████████████████████████

███████████████████████████████

███████████████████████████████

███████████ got my attention, but whatever our ideological stances and convictions, we were still dealing with abstractions, like one of those situational ethics exercises from a few decades earlier. After all, the war against Al Qaeda had barely begun. Journalists weren't even of one mind on how to spell the group's name.

In about the same timeframe, Tom Taylor, the army deputy general counsel, visited NCIS, the air force Office of Special Investigations (OSI), and some of the other agencies at CID headquarters at Fort Belvoir, Virginia. He informed us that, by President Bush's order of November 13, 2001, the army investigative branch, CID, would have the overall responsibility for war crimes and related offenses against the US by Al Qaeda or the Taliban. That didn't knock us out of the interrogation game, but it did give NCIS lower priority in getting in to see detainees and fulfilling our mission of moving them toward military trials and obtaining counterintelligence information. I would have been more depressed by the news if there hadn't been such constant flux all around us, but things were changing at such a high rate of speed that I figured they would change yet again, this time in our favor, and we could reestablish our credentials and employ our expertise at the new landing pad for the most important detainees: Guantanamo Bay, a place that Defense Secretary Donald Rumsfeld had just promised would house "the worst of the worst" prisoners being seized in Afghanistan, Iraq, and elsewhere.

CHAPTER 4

CARIBBEAN *WASTA*

American planes aren't allowed in Cuban airspace, so flights to Guantanamo always end in a hard right turn. One minute I was passing the island with a gorgeous view of the Caribbean stretching off toward Jamaica; the next all I could see out my window was ocean rushing toward me. The ten-seater C-12 banked steeply, turned 180 degrees, and approached the southwest corner of Cuba from the south.

We landed on Leeward Point Field. Outside sat a very hot tarmac, and then a mile or so past the airfield, the grass and shrubs began climbing up the Sierra Maestra, the largest mountain range in Cuba. I hopped into a waiting car and drove down to the ferry landing.

Guantanamo Bay divides the base, although almost everything except the airstrip is on the east side. We drove onto the ferry, and I walked up to the deck for a seat with a view of the tropical base to see what had changed since my last visit there in the 1990s. The breeze was wet and salty. Northward up the bay sat dozens of tiny islands dotting the water until it turned back into Cuban territory.

The United States has occupied Guantanamo since 1898, following the defeat of the Spanish by American and Cuban revolutionary forces. The US turned the rest of Cuba over to the revolutionaries but demanded that they lease the land around the natural harbor for a naval base. Reluctantly, the Cubans agreed. Guantanamo became forty-five square miles of water and land with its own acronym and shorthand pronunciation. The history of Gitmo has been complicated ever since.

Following the country's Communist takeover with Fidel Castro's victory in 1959, some Cubans fled to Gitmo, seeking asylum and making the base a permanent thorn in the side of the Castro regime. The US and Cuba began planting huge gardens of cacti and land mines to seal their respective borders, creating the second-largest minefield in the world. In the 1960s Castro accused the US of not paying for fresh water that flowed into the camp from Cuban territory. In response, the navy built a huge desalination plant and removed a chunk of the pipe that went into Cuba. And so it has gone ever since—a never-ending tit-for-tat, often petty stuff but sometimes deadly serious, as I was reminded by the navy patrol boat with a large-caliber gun mounted on the front that shot by us as we were about halfway across the bay.

After about a twenty-minute crossing, the ferry docked on the east side of Guantanamo Bay. A five-minute walk along the water's edge would take one to Fisherman's Point, the spot where Christopher Columbus had landed in Cuba more than 500 years earlier. Farther up the hill was a large windowed building. It had been used as the intel collection center in the 1950s. That's where the NCIS office was. During the Cold War, Guantanamo had been the only US naval base in a Communist country. NCIS agents would run along the shoreline trying to get pictures of the antennae arrays of the Soviet fleet as they sailed by. But in the post-Soviet world of satellite imagery, Gitmo's intel value had become diminished.

In the 1990s Gitmo was used as an international no-man's-land to hold Cuban and Haitian refugees seeking asylum in the United States. The flow of refugees quickly overwhelmed the vetting process. The camps around the base became tent cities surrounded by fences with concertina wire and guard towers. There were riots due to desperate conditions, so Camp X-Ray was established in the far northeast corner of Guantanamo. It was a crude, temporary jail just meant to separate the troublemakers from the rest of the camp.

The Pentagon created a multi-branch team called Joint Task Force 160 to keep order within those camps. I had been down to Guantanamo in the '90s as a member of the NCIS Hostage Negotiation Mobile Training Team but hadn't been back since.

Guantanamo was beautiful and historic, but Gitmo wasn't the most high-profile naval base. The people who wanted the action were on bases in places like the Philippines and Bahrain, or naval shipyards and marine bases. The pace at Guantanamo was more like Key West South. It was comfortable, with the only Baskin-Robbins, Subway, and McDonald's in Cuba. There was also a golf course that looked like a slightly grassier version of the moon—everyone carried around a small piece of AstroTurf to put under their ball. The pace was relatively relaxed and . . . Caribbean. You clocked in, did your job, and then went fishing or diving.

Now its unique location was bringing Gitmo a new mission. The Pentagon was going to reactivate JTF-160 and Camp X-Ray to deal with a different kind of prisoner. Gitmo is a hard base to get to, especially considering it is on an island just ninety miles from Florida. It is both the oldest overseas US military installation and the only one in a country with which the United States had no diplomatic ties. After more than a century, Cuba still rejects the legitimacy of the base's existence. But that was the point. Gitmo was a legal no-man's-land, making it a perfect spot for detaining a new category of prisoner.

Back up at the Navy Yard in DC, I had to admit there was a lot to like about the idea of a special interrogation zone at Gitmo for Rumsfeld's worst of the worst. Of course, I wasn't crazy about the FBI and NCIS taking a backseat to the army CID. But experience still counted, and we at NCIS—and the FBI, for that matter— had a ton of it to offer. True, the army would have the final say on things, but I knew for a fact that CID lacked any counterintelligence or counterterrorism expertise, or any meaningful experience in terrorism investigations or operations. We had all that, and I was confident our expertise would be needed in a common cause, and because Guantanamo was a naval base, NCIS already had a presence there, a nice leg up. I got busy developing a plan for us to expand our presence to accommodate the new detainees. We would need more physical space, more agents, and a broader skill set to meet our investigative and counterintelligence responsibilities.

Finding Al Qaeda operatives was the most critical job. Even though many of the prisoners were originating from a country where Pashto and Dari were the main languages, I needed Arabic speakers—the common language of Al Qaeda's inner circle—with extensive Middle East interrogation and counterintelligence experience. Fortunately, the USS *Cole* task force had included numerous pros who fit that bill. I felt Guantanamo detainees might even possess information useful in that investigation.

As part of the USS *Cole* investigation, we had developed culturally specific interrogation methods. For example, *wasta* is an Arabic term without an exact English translation. The meaning ranges from "nepotism" to "clout" to "connections." For example, if you asked someone how they got tickets to a sold-out show, they might just respond, "Wasta." Ultimately, it's a way of getting things done. This kind of Middle Eastern Arab cultural knowledge would also be very important to how we got information from detainees at Gitmo.

The average interview and interrogation approaches American law enforcement use don't have this background and insight, a big disadvantage in trying to get a confession or other information from Middle Eastern Arabs. Take the difference between guilt and shame. In the West, and also in parts of the Far East, we live in guilt-based societies. A Western suspect might feel guilty about what he did. Guilt is held inside him; it can begin to eat them up. The best way to relieve this internal guilt is to let it out and admit to the crime. The interrogator's job is to make this as easy as possible. He might, for example, suggest that extenuating circumstances played a role in the crime as a way of encouraging the subject to relieve his guilt.

But as we had learned during the USS *Cole* investigation, this approach doesn't play so well in Middle East Arab cultures. Their culture is not guilt-, but shame-based. The main motivation of detainees at Gitmo would be to avoid bringing shame on themselves and, by extension, their family, tribe, or terrorist brothers-in-arms. In a shame-based society, an undisclosed crime doesn't eat away at someone from the inside. In fact, it's the opposite. As long as the crime is hidden, it will not create shame. Offering a safe place for absolution is not effective. So what approach would work?

Not guilt, for sure. Not threats, either. Or screaming and shouting, or any of the other standards of movie and TV interrogations. In practice—as opposed to on-screen—those techniques are likely to make a detainee feel shamed and thus more resistant. What worked best with suspects beyond any doubt was a rapport-based approach.

This often takes an enormous amount of patience and time. Initially, the interrogator may spend hours in a room listening to the suspect talk about, say, his native country. Instead of coming in and firing off direct questions, such as, "Where is bin Laden hiding?" the interrogator tries to find commonalities, based on families, wives, education, etc. Eventually—maybe days or weeks later—the interrogator creates a relationship strong enough that he or she can leverage it for information. This may be a quid pro quo situation. Say the interrogator grants the detainee a wish, such as sending a letter home, or offers him fruit or tea. Using the theory of reciprocity, he can ask for something in return. The suspect may view maintaining his personal relationship with the interrogator as more important than withholding information.

Basically, this all amounted to shared helpfulness, as opposed to shared helplessness. We wouldn't play tough guy at Gitmo because, quite simply, it doesn't work. To get things started, I invited three of the top behavioral science specialists in the business—my good friend Mike Gelles, CIA psychologist ███████████, and ███████, a psychiatrist—to join my team as we developed a game plan for training our staff at Guantanamo. If it had worked with the Al Qaeda operatives in the USS *Cole* investigation, it would work there.

While I was working up in DC putting together our team for Gitmo, General Donald Ryder, the commander of the army CID, had called me in for a meeting. He was a critical figure, the top guy at the division in charge of conducting criminal investigations of the Gitmo detainees.

The following day, I walked into the army CID headquarters

and saw its slogan hanging on the wall: Do WHAT HAS TO BE DONE. *Hmm,* I thought. *It's not exactly "Veritas"*—the NCIS motto.

Inside the general's conference room, I saw a few people I knew from the FBI and the air force's OSI. But the presentation itself was by and for the army. It began with a talk about doctrine and went on from there. It was command and control on steroids.

When I got back to NCIS headquarters, I briefed director Dave Brant and his leadership group. Dave doesn't look particularly charismatic on first glance—he's a lanky guy with a brown mustache—but he's endlessly inquisitive, he never stops searching for different perspectives, and he's the kind of boss good people just love working under. He also doesn't have much tolerance for BS, especially when it comes to briefings.

"The task force they envision would put the FBI under army officers," I said, looking around the table. "Everybody knows that would be a nonstarter for the Bureau. And a system that marginalizes the group with the most experience and intel dealing with Al Qaeda . . ." I paused. "From my perspective, it's a mistake."

The director's conference room was silent. I assumed everyone was thinking the same things: How would it affect NCIS? The DOD? And, more important, what did it mean for what was now called the Global War on Terror? Would it hurt our chances of stopping the next attack?

Brant was still looking at me.

"They're going to fail," I said.

The director then went around the room with his eyes, giving each of his senior staff a chance to speak. No one said a thing.

"So you're telling me," he said, "that CID is going to take over jurisdiction from the FBI, and DOD is going to take over jurisdiction from the DOJ, to bring terrorists to justice, before some judicial process that has yet to be established?"

"Yes."

"And you think they will fail?"

I nodded.

"Then you'd better go down and help them! Mark, you have as much experience as anyone investigating terrorists and running task forces. Help them figure it out."

Then he walked off to call Donald Ryder, to get the ball rolling.

I showed up at CID offices the next morning and reported to Ryder. He smiled briefly when I walked in.

"Mark," he said. "CID doesn't have anyone with your type of meaningful experience investigating terrorists."

"Yes, sir."

"We're going to rely on NCIS and OSI to assist with the task force investigations."

"Glad to help."

And that quickly, I was on loan to the army—to help set up the new Criminal Investigation Task Force—CITF, pronounced "Sit-if." Technically, it was very similar to the work I'd been doing with NCIS, except CITF was under the army, the branch given the lead in these investigations. Instead of trying to jockey my way into the game with NCIS, CITF would be in charge of bringing terrorists to justice at Guantanamo. And we would be able to operate on a totally separate chain of command from Joint Task Force 160. They were in charge of the day-to-day world of running the detention center; CITF had a purely investigative role at Gitmo. Once I had set up the task force and someone was picked as deputy commander for CITF, the plan was that I'd return to my job at NCIS as the deputy assistant director.

After about a week on the job, I had another meeting with Ryder. I'd been pushing hard during those first days. Our job, as I saw it, was to get things done, not to wait for every small decision to travel up and down the chain of command, and I knew I had stepped on some toes and violated army customs while trying to push things forward. Was Ryder going to pull me back now? Hardly. In this follow-up meeting, he asked me to be brutally honest with him, and I had plenty to say. I laid out the cultural issues, structural issues, training issues, and operational issues we were facing.

"I need someone who can think outside the box on this one," said Ryder.

"You need someone who can throw it away!" I said. "Redesign the task force from scratch. It's got to be based on the mission, not some army force structure model."

As I continued, Ryder listened and occasionally gave a slight tilt of his head. When I was done, he said, "I got it. Now will you stay? I'm not sure we can do this mission without you. Will you stay on as my deputy commander?"

This would be the assignment of a lifetime, but it didn't feel right to take the position myself. I'd been detailed to Gen. Ryder to get the ball rolling, and I didn't want anyone thinking I had been lobbying myself into the deputy commander's slot. What to do? I couldn't say yes, but I couldn't turn it down outright.

"I work for Dave Brant," I finally said. "I do what he tells me."

Ryder got up from his conference table and told his secretary, "Get me Dave Brant, please."

The general walked to his desk and picked up the phone. I strained to hear, but all I could pick up was Ryder's soft-spoken confidence. There were bits and pieces about the "importance of the mission" and the "inherent challenges." Ryder then extended the phone toward me and said, "He wants to talk to you."

I grabbed the receiver. "You willing to stay?" asked Dave Brant.

"Absolutely."

"Good luck."

I handed the phone back to Ryder. After he thanked Brant, we returned to the conference table.

"My turn to brief you," he said. "I'm not an investigator—my first real exposure to CID was as its commanding general. Day-to-day operations are going to be under your control."

After telling Ryder how proud and honored I was to be placed in this position, he gave one last piece of guidance: "Take care of your people."

On the way out the door I said, "I'm going to have to break some china."

Ryder smiled and said, "Got it."

Even with the CITF lead role, I couldn't do everything my way. I wanted to set up our headquarters in a space in Crystal City, Virginia. There were a bunch of spaces there that were already outfitted as Sensitive Compartmented Information Facilities (SCIF) where we could receive and discuss highly classified information. But "the army way" won out. We moved into a converted motor pool warehouse on an army base in Fort Belvoir. It was basically a giant white shed. When I first walked into the shed, I could see a bunch of dead pigeons sprawled in the back on the concrete slab floor. I had a huge budget, though, and in less than two months we had totally SCIF-ed out the building. Now you couldn't enter the shed without going through a door with tumbler locks and another with a palm scanner.

We also did a total overhaul on the CITF structure, designing it to be less focused on staff and rank and more focused on results. I wanted experienced operators in key positions, not staff officers arranged in a bureaucratic hierarchy. And damned if I hadn't gotten them: our team built counterintelligence and counterterrorism experience into the very heart of the operation. I couldn't have been more proud of them, or more certain we would play a key role in preventing future attacks and ultimately helping to capture top Al Qaeda and bring them and other detainees to justice before military commissions.

To make sure everyone working at Gitmo was versed in Middle Eastern culture, mind-set, society, and interrogation protocols, I sent a ruddy-faced Arabic speaker, Bob McFadden, and Mike Gelles down to Guantanamo. I had known Bob since his first day on the job at the NCIS office in Philadelphia, where I was his first boss, and I had known Mike since his NCIS agent training. We all had worked together ever since.

Not only had Bob been extensively tutored in Arabic, but he'd also lived in the Middle East. Rapport building came easily to him. Mike, the NCIS chief psychologist, was different; he was an intense guy—on the surface almost Bob's opposite. It was hard to imagine Gelles as a psychologist treating patients, as he'd just as soon tell someone to "shut the fuck up" than pass them a box of tissues. But Gelles was sent down to Gitmo to explain the patience required when talking with associative thinkers, something he was very good at. Gelles trained our interrogators that Arabs tend to be associative thinkers. They may move from idea to idea, unlike Westerners, who are more likely to think in a sequential, goal-oriented, linear manner.

For example, say a subject named Omar mentions his Uncle Ahmed. The interrogator wants to know specifics: How old is Ahmed? Where does he live? Is he a devout Muslim? Does he have any links to Al Qaeda? Meanwhile, Omar starts talking about how "Uncle Ahmed used to like to give us dates under this fig tree behind his house."

It's easy for Westerners to view this as deception: *Why isn't he answering the question?* But it's not necessarily. The subject is talking about something that associates with his uncle. When dealing with an associative thinker, an interrogator needs to be more of a sponge and a collector. If Omar is talking, don't cut it off. It might not be the response to your immediate query, but it could be the answer to a question you don't yet know.

The flip side of this is that suspects who are actually linked to Al Qaeda may have received training that tried to weld linear thinking—say, a linear cover story—on minds that are trained to be associative. When suspects try to repeat these cover stories, they often come off as very rote and mechanistic. It would be like learning a Bruce Springsteen song on guitar and then being asked to play it backward. For associative thinkers, these awkward responses can be more indicative of deception than seemingly wandering stories.

Bob McFadden talked to our CITF team about Al Qaeda hierarchy and doing Al Qaeda interrogations from his years investigating and handling sources in the Middle East. All the people we sent down to Gitmo had prior interview and interrogation training; most were highly experienced. But to make sure they were ready for this challenge, we developed an investigative training program consisting of programs such as "The Middle Eastern Mindset," "al-Qaeda/Taliban," "al-Qaeda Life Cycle," "the al-Qaeda Training Manual," "Psychological Impact of Captivity," "Indicators for Potential Violence," "Interviewing, Elicitation, Interview and Interrogation Strategies," "Special Areas of Investigative Interest," and "the Consultation Model."

The training was intense, but the message behind it was simple: to succeed as an interrogator, you have to understand where the person you are interviewing is coming from—what his culture is like, what works and does not work with someone whose entire life experience might be radically different from your own. What could be more basic than that?

There were two other key factors stressed with our people. First was the need to ensure they didn't get emotionally overwhelmed or carried away. The heat of the moment, the memory of what had happened on 9/11—all of this could boil over in a hurry. But we had studied how Nazi war criminals were brought to justice at the Nuremburg trials after World War II for inhumane treatment of prisoners. Simply being a soldier following orders is no excuse for committing crimes. If there was evidence of any abuse of detainees, they needed to immediately report it, both because it was the right thing to do and because eventually it would come out in the open anyway.

"There are no secrets," I told every member of my team. "Only delayed disclosures."

CHAPTER 5

DIRT FARMERS

Camp X-Ray had been a fairly crude detention center when it was put together in the mid-1990s to house disruptive and criminal refugees. It was way off in the far corner of the camp, almost in Cuba. When the camp was reactivated on January 11, 2002, the Australian David Hicks became one of the first residents. John Walker Lindh never joined him there; Lindh was instead transported to the USS *Bataan* and then back to the States for trial. Our CITF people did debrief him on several occasions and found him to be quite helpful in mapping his travels through Afghanistan and describing the people he met along the way. In fact, we kept the map he drew for us, with his hand-written notes, on the wall in our CITF conference room.

David Hicks had plenty of company, though, even without Lindh. In the first six months after Camp X-Ray reopened, roughly one hundred new detainees arrived each month, nearly all from Afghanistan. All of them were housed in blocks of outdoor mesh cages made out of fencing material. They looked like dog pens, but the military wouldn't even allow their working dogs to be kept in un-air-conditioned pens like that. Each cage had two buckets, one for drinking water, the other a toilet. There were about a dozen such blocks, surrounded by multiple chain-link fences with weeds growing under them and concertina wire playing across the top. Plywood guard stations with American flags nailed to the side stood watch. It was sort of like a high-security, low-rent zoo. By February 2002 it was also getting overcrowded. We asked for better facilities but were told to "hang tight" because Gitmo was just a temporary holding site.

When Bob McFadden first arrived at the camp, he walked past the guard station into Camp X-Ray, then paused for a second to take it all in before saying, "This is a bizarre scene."

I'd been down to Gitmo on and off since it opened, so I served as Bob's tour guide, warning him to avoid the camp's eccentric characters. One poor guy nicknamed Wild Bill would chuck his shit or piss at you if you got too close. Another guy we nicknamed Waffle Butt because he pressed his bare ass up against the mesh any time someone got near.

None of that threw Bob for a loop. He'd been inside plenty of other nasty places, but as soon as the detainees realized Bob spoke Arabic, they began yelling at him: "Please, please, Mister, Mister! There's been a mistake! There was a mix-up."

Bob talked to some of them a bit, and as he did so, I could see his face getting more and more troubled. Finally, he grabbed a list of detainees, scanned the names, looked at the mass of prisoners in front of him, and shouted out, "What the fuck? Who are these guys? None of them are Arabs!"

The detainee list was full of Afghan and Pakistani names such as Iqbal, Khan, and Ahmadzia. Whoever they were, they weren't part of the core Al Qaeda network—the Egyptians, Saudis, and other Arabs we'd been tracking for years.

While Bob was standing in the middle of Camp X-Ray's over-crowded holding pens, US helicopters were flying over Afghanistan making sure they would stay full. The primary goal of invading Afghanistan in the fall of 2001 was capturing bin Laden and his inner circle. That hadn't happened, of course. By January 2002, bin Laden was almost certainly already in Pakistan, where he would be captured almost a decade later, DOA: dead on arrival. But our military hadn't given up on the chase, only broadened it: Helicopters were still dropping flyers offering bounties for capture of members of the Taliban or Al Qaeda. One read (translated into English):

> Get wealth and power beyond your dreams. . . . You can receive millions of dollars helping the anti-Taliban forces catch al-Qaida and Taliban murderers. This is enough money to take care of your family, your village, your tribe for the rest of your life. Pay for livestock and doctors and school books and housing for all your people.

They may not have been totally accurate, but the flyers were effective. Most of the people who ended up at Gitmo were picked up by the Northern Alliance or other groups that didn't necessarily have any interest in the global war on terror, aside from picking up a $5,000 per head bounty. The result was an explosion of human trafficking in the Hindu Kush mountains. The Northern Alliance would jam so many detainees into Conex shipping containers that they started to die of suffocation. Not wanting to lose their bounties, the captors sprayed the tops of the boxes with machine guns to open ventilation holes. A lot of these prisoners were actually looking forward to being handed over to the Americans, figuring it would be pretty obvious they weren't Al Qaeda. Instead, they ended up on Caribbean vacations—minus the resorts, lazy afternoons by the pool, and rum cocktails.

But beyond the bounty-driven roundup of detainees who had the misfortune of running into Northern Alliance troops, the vetting process for determining who might be a terrorist was simply nonfunctional. Mere possession of a rifle or visiting a guesthouse where Al Qaeda operatives were thought to have stayed could be interpreted as someone aiding and abetting the enemy. Even people known to have been conscripted into the Taliban at gunpoint and who then surrendered to the US alliance were seen as security threats. But it got even more ridiculous. Because some terrorists had used an internationally popular model of Casio digital wristwatch as a timer for bombs, wearing one of these watches became suspect. (True, bin Laden had been photographed wearing one, but NCIS director Dave Brant also sported one.) And not just suspect: there were actually detainees held at Gitmo because they had been wearing a Casio watch.

This was not what I signed up for. When I was setting up the task force, I was promised "the worst of the worst." There were to be a limited number of detainees, and they would all be targets for prosecution or high-value intel exploitation. But in our initial assessment interviews with detainees, it became clear that Bob was right. We'd ended up with a bunch of guys warlords had turned in for a bounty with no evidence they had any value. We called them dirt farmers—lots and lots of dirt farmers.

By mid-February, the makeshift Guantanamo prison was reaching maximum capacity with these low-value detainees. They didn't belong there, they were taking up space, and they were making our job a helluva lot more difficult. We couldn't keep up with the influx. Everyone from Rumsfeld down knew we needed to release some of them. The Pentagon even sent a contingent of lawyers to meet with a CENTCOM deputy commander, Michael "Rifle" DeLong, and ask him to slow or stop the flow of no-value prisoners into Guantanamo. DeLong was a hard-nosed three-star marine corps general I had worked with in Italy, and he was used to getting his way.

"We're warfighters," DeLong said. "We don't have the luxury of detaining prisoners forward." Becoming a jailor, he told his visitors, was an impediment to his military mission. Instead, DeLong informed the lawyers there were even more prisoners in the pipeline.

His sentiment was somewhat understandable because, while detaining suspects was a small part of his mission, the big bounties being paid for prisoners was compromising larger concerns. But his problem was quickly becoming our problem too. When we became the primary destination for DeLong's teeming hundreds, what had been designed as a secretive intel-gathering location became a holding pen. Except people—and animals—get released from holding pens regularly. Gitmo wasn't designed for quick turnaround—it took a lot of paperwork and a blessing from all the way up the chain of command. The JTF-160 commander, a no-nonsense marine named Michael Lehnert, was unimpressed. "It takes an army captain to send someone to Gitmo," he said, "and the President of the United States to get them out."

Because of CITF's status as an investigative organization within the DOD, we could share our information with our international counterparts—something the CIA and FBI often either couldn't or wouldn't do. These relationships also allowed us to get some no-value detainees out of Gitmo and repatriated, even though that required going all the way up the chain of command and through multiple inter-agency reviews.

In late January 2004, I attended a luncheon at the Washington, DC, residence of the Belgian ambassador. It is a huge building with a horseshoe driveway. As I pulled in, the attaché, Luc, approached me and told me to leave my government car in front of the embassy and waved me toward a tuxedoed server holding a tray of drinks. During lunch, the ambassador asked me what he needed to do to get two of our Belgian detainees back.

"I'm just an investigator," I explained, "not a policymaker. So I can't speak for the Pentagon or the State Department. But I can definitely let the secretary of defense's lawyers know you want your people back."

A little while later, the attaché, Luc, walked over to me and asked if he could borrow my keys to move the car.

Back at CITF, I made some enquiries about the Belgians. Turned out we had no case on them, there was no intel value, and the Pentagon agreed we should release them back to Belgium.

I called Luc. "Looks good. The ball is rolling to get your guys back home."

"Great," said Luc. "Did you check your trunk?"

Oh shit, I thought. *What did he do?*

It turned out he'd put two cases of Belgian beer in the trunk. When I reported it to the Pentagon, they started joking that I had traded detainees for two cases of beer!

In February, as we were trying to stem the flow of detainees who didn't belong at Guantanamo, we got word that the army was creating a new joint task force, JTF-170, to take over intel gathering. The exact wording of JTF-170's mission was something like "global focal point for interrogation operations for all government agencies under Operation Enduring Freedom." I wasn't sure exactly what it meant—I don't think anyone was—but as I interpreted it, CITF would continue to do criminal investigations even as we helped to collect intel that would enhance the new JTF-170's total product. Meanwhile, the old task force, JTF-160, would remain in charge of detention activities, everything from facility management to feeding the detainees. How the actual lineup of responsibilities panned out would depend on who was picked to lead JTF-170, and here Secretary of Defense Donald Rumsfeld seemed to have made a curious choice: Army Major General Michael Dunlavey.

For one, Dunlavey was a reservist from Erie, Pennsylvania—not an active-duty officer. Second, Dunlavey had done his drilling in signal intelligence (SIGINT) at the NSA. SIGINT includes things such as analyzing intercepted cell phone calls. His training had very little to do with the human intelligence (HUMINT) collections we were doing at Guantanamo. Why exactly Rumsfeld personally selected him for the job, I don't know; there were plenty of active duty officers with experience in HUMINT.

It took only a week after Dunlavey arrived on base for the first signs of potential trouble to surface. The general introduced himself to one of my CITF members by pointing to the two stars on his collar.

"I'm here now, and I'm in charge!" Dunlavey said.

Of course, we all knew who he was. We were there to support him. But most of us were civilians with a different chain of command. We didn't answer to Dunlavey. Like anyone wearing civvies—a polo shirt and khakis for me—we weren't supposed to salute when Dunlavey or any other officer walked by. This was probably part of the problem. We would find out that he seemed to have an obsessive need for everyone to recognize his authority. Just one example: Because there are detainees at Gitmo, everyone covers up their name on their uniform to protect their identities. Dunlavey bucked that rule, covering his name but making sure the detainees could see his two stars—the only two stars on the base.

He was also defensive about his lack of background in gathering human intelligence. "I was in 'Nam," Dunlavey barked out of the side of his mouth. "I know how to do interrogations!"

Uh-oh, I thought. *I don't remember much good coming out of those.* They hadn't gotten much intel or treated prisoners so well.

We'd also received word through back channels at NSA that Dunlavey's obsessions ran deeper than control issues. After a month of trips down to Gitmo, I was beginning to agree. The guy seemed a bit of a loon.

Early on, someone at the base joked to him that he was number three on the Al Qaeda hit list. He apparently took it so seriously that he demanded NCIS provide a security detail for him and his wife—as if they needed any more precautions on a US naval base filled with servicemen on an island in the Caribbean. We gave him and his wife some body armor, telling Dunlavey, "Wear this if you're really worried."

I found out he had a pair of nickel-plated pistols flown down to Gitmo, even though he couldn't carry them on the base. These were personal weapons, not issued by the military. Maybe he was posing with them in front of his mirror, pretending to be Patton? The NCIS agents assigned to the CITF took possession of the pistols "for safekeeping" and locked them in a weapons safe. He got his handguns back when his assignment at Gitmo was over.

One night, as I was having drinks with a few other CITF people at the base's tiki bar and enjoying the stunning view of the bay, Dunlavey pulled up with his car windows down and the Pointer Sisters song "I'm So Excited" blaring. Nothing against his music choice, but this was not the behavior anyone expected from a commanding general, especially one at the "global focal point for interrogations for all government agencies under Operation Enduring Freedom."

Taken bit by bit, Dunlavey's actions might have seemed merely bizarre or silly, but he wasn't just one of those annoying managers you want to avoid in the elevator. He was the commanding general at a military facility during an unpredictable global war. When people on the base started calling Dunlavey Cocoa Puffs—after the cereal's ad line "I'm cuckoo for Cocoa Puffs"—you could tell discipline was at risk of breaking down. In fact, people were even making references to a movie where just that dynamic was taken to extremes. When Dunlavey was out of earshot, staff would ask, "Where are my strawberries?"—a joking reference to the mentally unstable Captain Queeg in *The Caine Mutiny*.

There were other, more substantial, areas of conflict between CITF and Dunlavey. We had just completed a major operation, in which a detainee provided critical and actionable intelligence on a location in Afghanistan. In exchange, he was allowed a phone call home to let his family know he was alive. The operation took months to pull together and was coordinated with multiple organizations, including the Defense Intelligence Agency, CIA, and the NSA. It was an excellent example of how all the intel groups at Gitmo—CITF, FBI, and JTF-170—could work together to produce actionable intelligence from a detainee. It was also a perfect example of rapport building and reciprocity.

We were all damn proud of it—not just for the intel but as yet another vindication of our approach. Soon afterward, though, ██, called me at my office in Fort Belvoir. "Dunlavey's lost it!"

Turns out, the commanding general was outraged that our highly successful effort hadn't been directed and controlled entirely by JTF-170. The general was accusing ██████, FBI supervisor ██████████████, and his own chief of staff, Donald Woolfolk, of conspiring against him. Dunlavey told ██████ that he was initiating an army 15-6 on him, a procedure used for noncriminal command-level investigations. There were three problems with that strategy. First, ███████ wasn't in the army. Second, he didn't work for JTF-170. Third, everyone knew it was a ridiculous claim.

"Get him out of the sun," I said to ██████. "It's baking his brain." Then I notified my superiors. In the end, General Donald Ryder—the head of army CID—called Dunlavey directly.

I waited until 5:30 PM the next day for the process to play out before calling over to Southern Command (SOUTHCOM), under whose aegis Gitmo fell. Brigadier General Ronald Burgess assured me that they had Dunlavey under control.

"It's bullshit," said Burgess, referring to Dunlavey's allegations. "It's done."

Unfortunately, it wasn't done. In fact, it was going to get a lot worse.

Not only was Camp X-Ray an uncomfortable spot for detainees, it was a horrible place for conducting interrogations. We had bribed the Seabees—the navy's construction crew—into building us our interrogation rooms with two cases of beer. You get what you pay for: They were basically four-sided plywood boxes with doors and a few chairs inside. The real problem was not the comfort level but the lack of privacy.

When you are conducting an interrogation, you don't want the other detainees to see you coming and going with your most recent subject. Some people just didn't talk (we called them "head hangers"). Even though we knew they weren't going to say anything, we couldn't let it be known that, by not talking, detainees could skip out on interrogations. We also didn't want the other detainees to know who was talking to us. So we'd just sit in the room for three hours with the head hangers, asking them a question every thirty minutes or so.

Generally speaking, Saudis were the biggest head hangers. They looked down at the Afghanis and Egyptians, and some refused to talk to us at all. But a Saudi national who arrived in mid-February was different. Identified as prisoner 063, he claimed he was involved in falconry and had simply gotten caught up when the ground operations began in Afghanistan. It was probably a cover story, but despite cries from JTF-170 that we needed to toughen up on him, we had faith in our rapport-based interrogation techniques, so we let him talk and talk until we had enough little bits and pieces to build a mosaic. Our task force and the FBI shared a large squad bay where we did link analysis by hand on huge sheets of paper taped to the walls. Link analysis tracks connections between nodes, and the more we looked into 063's connections, the more we realized he was one of our most valuable intel assets. Unfortunately, his potentially high value would also attract the manic attention of General Dunlavey.

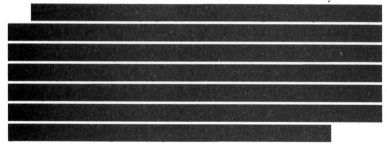

As we kept pressing, we found that al-Qahtani also fit into another line of inquiry. The INS had been doing an analysis of likely flight patterns consistent with those of other 9/11 hijackers. Al-Qahtani fit the profile, although he was hardly the only one who did.

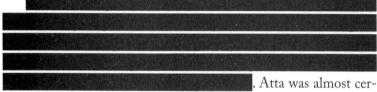

. Atta was almost certainly there to pick him up. Once al-Qahtani was detained and then deported, Atta left.

That was when the whole picture came together. The 9/11 attacks were carried out by nineteen men, but a growing body of evidence was suggesting there were supposed to be twenty. On three of the four flights that were hijacked, there were four "musclemen" who controlled the crew and one pilot. The fourth plane only had three musclemen, and it was also the only one that didn't hit its target. En route to a target in Washington, DC, it crashed into the ground in Shanksville, Pennsylvania, after the passengers revolted. We had likely found the twentieth 9/11 hijacker—the only living operative of the largest terror attack on US soil.

There was pressure on all sides to produce intel. Everybody wanted to know where bin Laden was or any information that might be used to thwart future attacks. The White House was also trying to justify an invasion of Iraq; they wanted info about Al Qaeda in Iraq—which, at the time, didn't exist—and where the fictitious Iraqi weapons of mass destruction were located. Even if he wasn't part of bin Laden's inner circle, al-Qahtani looked more promising than most of the dirt farmers at Gitmo. He could be very valuable in understanding how the attacks happened if we built up a rapport with him and developed him properly. But al-Qahtani had also caught the eye of Dunlavey, whose new JTF-170 was practicing a completely different art.

While CITF was packed with career federal agents, intelligence analysts, PhDs and lawyers, experts who had been doing this sort of thing for a living, the army used very junior staff, usually reservists in their early twenties, most of whom had never been in an interrogation room with a bad guy before.

I once asked one of the JTF-170 interrogators if he'd interviewed someone before. "Oh, yeah," he said, and pointed to his partner, whom he had role-played with during their training together at the army intelligence school in Fort Huachuca, Arizona. These were dedicated reservists, but it wasn't fair to expect them to go get information out of a suspected terrorist, someone who is purported to be the "worst of the worst."

When the reservists were called up, they first got shipped off to Fort Huachuca, where they learned the techniques described in the Army Field Manual—FM 34-52, "Intelligence Interrogation"—a program that wasn't grounded in any science and was mostly ineffective. More to the point for our immediate purposes, the techniques were definitely *not* designed to deal with a non-Western culture.*

While our CITF guys might be on the floor drinking tea and talking about soccer with a detainee to gain his confidence, the JTF-170 guys would be walking into a room with a shopping list of priority intelligence requirements. Some walked in with an exaggerated swagger. One guy even wore a full cowboy outfit into the interrogation session, including a vest and chaps.

But once they got to the table and tried to stare down a detainee, the JTF-170 guys didn't have much left. The JTF-170

---

* To its credit, though, the FM 34-52 interrogation protocols were at least humane and rapport-based. Witness this sample:

The approach phase actually begins when the interrogator first comes in contact with the source and continues until the prisoner begins answering questions pertinent to the objective of the interrogation effort. Interrogators do not "run" an approach by following a set pattern or routine. Each interrogation is different, but all approaches in interrogations have the following purposes in common:

Establish and maintain <u>control</u> over the source and the interrogation.

Establish and maintain rapport between the interrogator and the source.

Manipulate the source's emotions and weaknesses to gain his willing cooperation.

interrogators would sit down with the list of twenty questions their superior had developed. Asking the questions was the plan, and the interrogators were going to follow out their orders. The results might be something like this:

JTF-170 Interrogator: Do you know Abu Zubaydah?

Translator: Do you know Abu Zubaydah?

Detainee: No.

Translator: No.

Interrogator: Where did you first meet Abu Zubaydah?

Translator: Where did you first meet Abu Zubaydah?

Detainee: I already told you, I don't know Abu Zubaydah.

Translator: I already told you, I don't know Abu Zubaydah.

Interrogator: How many people were there when you met Abu Zubaydah?

Translator: How many people were there when you met Abu Zubaydah?

Detainee: Are you translating this properly? Did you not tell him that I don't know Abu Zubaydah?

And so on for twenty questions. The detainees got frustrated. The translators got frustrated, and maybe even sympathetic to the detainees. But the interrogators continued doggedly down the whole list. They needed answers because those were the requirements. Finally, a detainee would put his head down and shut up. Out of ideas, the interrogators would leave the room and check in with their supervisors. They'd develop a new interrogation plan and start again. It was a completely wooden command-and-control process that didn't give the interrogators half a chance to succeed. The JTF-170 would inevitably conclude that their techniques were not working because the detainees had some sort of training to resist interrogation. It always seemed to work when they role-played interrogations with each other.

We wanted to try to help these guys on JTF-170. If they were successful, it could only benefit us. We normally ran interrogations with one FBI guy and one CITF guy in a room at a time. But we decided we'd do "tiger teams" and include the JTF-170 team interrogators as well. Unfortunately, their training was so different it proved an impossible fit. The army interrogators, basically conscripts, would walk into a room for the first time thinking the detainee was just waiting to be cracked open and they were the next Jack Bauer. But week after week, they got nothing useful. The detainees also got sick of the pointless questioning. Instead of answering the questions, they would start to chant and pray. Attempting to reassert control, the interrogators would duct tape their mouths— further guaranteeing they wouldn't get any information—and so it would go.

Unfortunately, JTF-170 had a very attractive excuse for their interrogation failures. In 2000 a computer file had been found during a raid on the house of a suspected terrorist in Manchester, England. On the file was a manual that reportedly laid out how terrorists should wage war. The Pentagon claimed it was an Al Qaeda manual for training its members. Among the tactics discussed (in what became known as the Manchester Document) were details on what treatment to expect if captured—as well as advice on resisting and lying to captors. When detainees at Guantanamo refused to cooperate, interrogators with JTF-170 were quick to blame "classic Manchester resistance tactics!" The interrogators' inability to extract intel was not viewed as evidence that they needed to recalibrate their approach. Instead, it was taken as proof that the detainees were both Al Qaeda and trained to resist these methods of intel exploitation.

It was these same reputed Manchester Document tactics that inspired psychologists James Mitchell and Bruce Jessen, the CIA contractors, to write their paper on countermeasures to Al Qaeda resistance. For Mitchell and Jessen, the Manchester Document's training could be overcome by using the exploitative SERE training techniques to break down subjects. This paper led directly to the development of the CIA's enhanced interrogation techniques. At Guantanamo, the leadership at JTF-170 was drawing similar conclusions: they didn't need to get smarter; they needed to get *tougher*.

CHAPTER 6

BATTLE LAB

Our success with al-Qahtani only heightened General Dunlavey's frustration with the lack of information his team was getting out of detainees. He had noticed that our task force had its own Behavioral Science Consultation Team. The idea behind our BSCT—pronounced "biscuit"—was to improve our rapport-based interrogations by having a consulting group of psychologists and other professionals, such as Mike Gelles, ███████████, and Joseph Krofcheck.

Dunlavey decided his JTF-170 team needed that kind of expertise. But instead of asking for help from us, he built up his own team with inexperienced clinicians, which we called pseudo-BSCT. In early June 2002, Dunlavey had three people reassigned to Gitmo to staff his new team, including army clinical psychologist ████ ██████████ as well as psychiatrist Major Paul Burney. Neither of the doctors had any training or experience in interrogation. In fact, when they got off the plane at Gitmo, Burney and ████ were under the impression they were being assigned there to care for US service members dealing with battle-related stress.

██████ wasn't able to smoothly transition to his new job initially. Not long after arriving, the psychologist called up Larry James, his mentor at the Walter Reed National Military Medical Center in Bethesda, Maryland. ██████ said he was extremely uncomfortable in his unfamiliar role. According to James, ██████ sounded distraught and anxious. The pseudo-BSCT he had joined was planning how to introduce terror tactics into al-Qahtani's world.

James promised he'd get ██████ some help. He called up his colleague, psychologist Morgan Banks. The two were both concerned over ██████ lack of expertise, but James saw a positive side: As James wrote in his book, *Fixing Hell*, he and Banks had an opportunity "to do the right thing and influence the interrogation process, assuming [they] could get Major ██████ the appropriate training." Unfortunately, Banks agreed.

Banks wasn't just another clinician, but the military psychologist assigned to Fort Bragg, the place where the SERE program was first developed. Banks was working with the Special Operation forces that made up forward-deployed Special Mission Units. His predecessor had been James Mitchell, the psychologist entranced by Martin Seligman's concept of learned helplessness who, with Bruce Jessen, was one of the fathers of the CIA's enhanced interrogation techniques. Banks was a lower profile than Mitchell, but he was also an advocate for adopting the SERE techniques to interrogations.

There was one important distinction between them. Mitchell was a private contractor to the CIA—he had no contracts to provide interrogation theory or training to anyone in the defense department. Banks, though, was a well-positioned army officer promoting SERE techniques within the military. However, like

Mitchell and Jessen, Banks had no expertise in lawful interrogations. He arranged for ▮▮ and Burney to fly up to Fort Bragg to get their first training in SERE interrogation techniques. Because SERE was initially developed to help service members develop a resistance to the brutal treatment they could expect from foreign governments, the education ▮▮ and Burney received included harsh and illegal intel exploitation techniques. In fact, within the SERE community, "exploitation techniques" was the code phrase for torture.

On June 9, 2002, about a week after ▮▮ and Burney's arrival, I was on a plane down to Gitmo with my colleagues Ralph Blincoe and Mike Gelles. We were making the trip to try and squelch the growing enthusiasm for SERE-based interrogation. Since ▮▮ had arrived, CITF had been trying to nudge him in the opposite direction as Larry James, Morgan Banks, and Dunlavey. We wanted to make sure he knew about the proven rapport-building interrogation CITF used. But ▮▮ was still heading down the path favored by Dunlavey. With Morgan Banks's assistance, ▮▮ and Burney were planning to begin "psychological exploitation" of al-Qahtani. And they were doing so with techniques that looked suspiciously like Mitchell and Jessen's EITs. In a sense, they were serving a similar role as Mitchell and Jessen, but instead of providing medical cover for torture in the CIA, they were doing so in the DOD. The programs they were developing also owed a debt to Martin Seligman's concept of learned helplessness. Of course, Seligman had observed learned helplessness in dogs that had received a constant battery of electric shocks. ▮▮ and Burney were designing treatment for human beings.

Once we landed at Guantanamo and got across the bay, Blincoe and I went up the hill to JTF-170's headquarters to talk with Dunlavey. The trip was a waste; the general gave us the usual runaround.

Back down at CITF's office, I saw Mike Gelles walk in, hyperventilating. "I can't believe these psychologists are getting directly involved in interrogations. They're actually advocating for using SERE and that learned helplessness shit," he fumed. He gripped the back of a chair. "They have no fucking experience! I almost feel sorry for them. They're gonna lose their licenses."

Gelles had more experience than anyone on the pseudo-BSCT. But like all our operational psychologists, he never participated in interrogations. Gelles explained his job as similar to an NFL offensive or defensive coordinator. He sat anonymously and high up in the box seats, observing plays from above, viewing activities through a different lens and giving those on the field a different perspective than they might see in the thick of the action. Medical professionals on the pseudo-BSCT were planning on being involved at all levels of the interrogation process.

I was personally pissed at Banks for the whole mess. When Mike and I had first heard Dunlavey was considering using SERE tactics for interrogation, we'd gotten in touch with Banks, who had advised us that the techniques were not appropriate. As interest in using SERE-based interrogation grew at Gitmo, I had used Banks's expert opinion to make the arguments that personnel involved in SERE training were not interrogators. Even in the controlled conditions at Fort Bragg, where both detainees and interrogators were American military personnel, abuses occurred. Much more serious abuses at Gitmo seemed an almost foregone conclusion. But now Banks had flipped his script. He was using his psychological expertise to train Gitmo personnel in breaking down detainees.

Whatever tactics JTF-170 was developing, they still had to wait to get their hands on al-Qahtani, and believe me, everyone wanted a piece. Given that we were the ones who had identified al-Qahtani

as a potentially high-value target for both intel and prosecution—
an actual worst of the worst—I was able to convince the Pentagon
to let CITF arrange a pecking order, and we put the FBI at the top
of it, mostly because I was familiar with ███████ from the USS
Cole investigation and thought he was the best possible person to
take on al-Qahtani.

█ had an amazing knack for developing rapport with subjects. He would sit on the floor with them and discuss politics or
religion in his fluent Arabic. In the spring of 2002, █ had used
his rapport-based techniques while interrogating a high-profile
detainee ███████ named Abu Zubaydah. During this time, Zubaydah gave up several important pieces of intel, including naming
Khalid Sheikh Mohammed as the 9/11 mastermind and disclosing
information about dirty bomber Jose Padilla.

In July 2002, █ and other FBI agents arrived at Gitmo, hoping to match their progress ███████, and initially, they made
some moderate progress in interrogating al-Qahtani—intel as well
as evidence—but eventually they hit a roadblock. Al-Qahtani shut
down and stopped talking. █ was sent home while the other FBI
investigators continued the interrogation.

This was the moment Dunlavey was waiting for. "Law enforcement had their chance," he said. "They failed. Now we need to get
serious."

Dunlavey realized al-Qahtani was potentially much more
valuable than what he called the "Mickey Mouse prisoners" at
Gitmo. Getting intel out of al-Qahtani would be a huge boost to
his career. Dunlavey's interrogators were claiming that Manchester
Document resistance techniques were stopping them from being
successful. The general was also convinced that the solution to his
intel exploitation problems was harsher measures. He believed getting tougher was the best way to get intel on Al Qaeda in Iraq,

prevent attacks, and save battlefield lives. Dunlavey proposed to have al-Qahtani "sent off island" to either Jordan, Egypt, or another third country. Basically, he wanted to do a CIA-style rendering of al-Qahtani to see what could be tortured out of him. ████████████

██

██

██

██

████████████████████████████████.

Then I got a call from Bill Lietzau, a high-ranking marine corps judge advocate assigned to the DOD office of general counsel working on detainee matters and the military commissions process.

"Mark, did the FBI ever run a rendition plan by you?" he asked.

"What?" I said. "Rendition for who?"

"They wanted to have al-Qahtani sent to Jordan for interrogation by local authorities." I closed my eyes.

What is happening? I thought. *The FBI was on our side fighting JTF-170 when they wanted to torture al-Qahtani. Now they want to do an end run around me? The premiere law enforcement agency in the United States is actually going to send a prisoner to be tortured?*

Once Lietzau got wind of the plan, he referred the FBI back to us. Lietzau knew it stank and that we wouldn't approve it. The FBI also knew we wouldn't approve it. To short-circuit Lietzau's resistance, the FBI took their case higher up the command chain to the office of Special Operations and Low Intensity Conflict (SOLIC), which oversees all special operations within the Pentagon. They found a receptive ear in Marshall Billingslea, the head of SOLIC. To counter their efforts, we brought in our own big gun, Major General Thomas Romig, the army's top lawyer. But Billingslea didn't slow down when Romig protested the interrogation procedures.

"Guys," he said. "It's time to wake up and smell the coffee. It's time to take the gloves off."

When Britt Mallow, the CEO of CITF, explained that SERE aren't interrogation techniques and simply don't work, Billingslea quickly replied: "You don't know what you're taking about."

Despite the support their idea got in the upper echelons of the military, the FBI never got to render al-Qahtani. In fact, it's not clear exactly where the idea originated. It's possible it began and ended with the FBI Guantanamo unit chief, but the FBI has kept those details a closely guarded secret. One thing was clear to me now: torturing detainees for intel was looked on favorably by some of the top brass in DOD and, at some levels, even within the FBI.

While I was pushing back on the aggressive interrogation of al-Qahtani at Gitmo, another event far above my pay grade in DC had already changed the playing field. On August 1, 2002, President Bush's lawyer, Alberto Gonzales, received a fifty-page memo from Assistant Attorney General John Yoo titled "Standards of Conduct for Interrogation under 18 U.S.C."

The first paragraph began to answer the question of what constitutes torture, specifically in terms of conduct outside the United States. Acts that were intended to "inflict severe pain or suffering" were illegal, claimed the legal team, before adding that they must be of an "extreme nature" to qualify as torture. If that didn't leave the door open wide enough, the next sentence declared that "certain acts may be cruel, inhuman and degrading" but not actually be considered torture.

The arguments continued in that vein until the last three pages of the memo, an appendix of activity that had been found to actually meet the definition of torture. This list included a man who was pistol-whipped into submission, given only a robe to wear, held for more than five years, forced to play Russian roulette, beaten, chained outside in winter, left in a rodent- and scorpion-infested cell, randomly beaten, and subjected to some unexplained surgical procedure. Other cases included a nun who was blindfolded, burned with cigarettes, and raped, and a man who was doused in gasoline and burned to death. This was indicative of the low bar the memo set for acceptable behavior. The opinion in the memo was passed to top lawyers at the CIA and Pentagon.

Because I didn't know about the August memo at the time, I just thought the enthusiasm some people at the Pentagon had for torture tactics was the result of being poorly informed. I figured they were acting stupidly because they didn't have the facts. Once the right professionals at CITF or NCIS, or even the FBI, educated people like Billingslea on what actually worked with detainees, things would settle down. I didn't know I was fighting against the White House.

Although explicit knowledge of the August memo was very exclusive, the result of the legal opinion echoed around the world. ███████████, the CIA took suspected Al Qaeda member Abu Zubaydah from the FBI interrogators and began so-called enhanced interrogation techniques on him. This kind of activity is hard to compartmentalize. Once torture is accepted in limited doses, it begins to spread like a virus.

By August 2002, JTF-170's intelligence collection was being looked at as a failure, and its shortcomings became the subject of an army investigation. JTF-170 was certainly a shambles, but the way the army went about fixing it was strange, if not suspicious. Army colonel John P. Custer was asked to lead the review. Colonel Custer was reputedly directly related to the more infamous General Custer. What was certain is that the colonel was the assistant commandant of Fort Huachuca, the place where JTF-170 interrogators were trained in field manual techniques. Why was the army sending Custer to evaluate what was essentially his own program? It was sort of like asking the fox to rebuild the chicken coup.

If you looked at the whole process a little cynically, however, it became less surprising when Custer agreed with Dunlavey's assessments. The colonel recommended that Dunlavey's pseudo-BSCT's methods could create the conditions that would be "conducive to extracting information by exploiting detainees' vulnerabilities." Given what I know now, it seems entirely possible that Custer was selected to "review" the program with the ultimate goal of amping up interrogation practices from the beginning. It certainly wouldn't be the first army investigation with a predetermined conclusion.

But Custer went one step further. Though JTF-160 had a more limited operation than it had when Gitmo had reopened in February, the group still operated independently, which undoubtedly drove the control-obsessed Dunlavey even more bonkers. What's worse, in Dunlavey's view, JTF-160 actually treated the detainees decently. President Bush had said that, though the Geneva Conventions didn't apply to them, those detained would be treated at conditions comparable to the Geneva Conventions. The marine general in charge, Michael Lehnert, had followed that order, as had his replacement, army general Rick Baccus. It wasn't a summer camp, but detainees had access to books, including Korans, and food that was appropriate for Muslims, including separate containers for meat and vegetables. Custer's second proposal gave Dunlavey another gift. He proposed merging JTF-160 and JTF-170 into JTF-GTMO, a new structure that gave one general total control over the operation.

Custer's last flourish became the best-known. In the report he filed on September 10, 2002, Custer called Guantanamo Bay

"America's Battle Lab." The next day, CITF's Britt Mallow met with Rumsfeld's counsel, Jim Haynes, to complain. Calling a prison and interrogation center a "lab" evoked unpleasant images of Nuremburg. It would further encourage the psychologists and psychiatrists on the pseudo-BSCT to experiment on detainees with untested techniques. Not only was that sort of behavior illegal, it was totally unscientific. Trying to determine whether something is effective on a live detainee when you're trying to exploit their intelligence is not how behavioral research works. CITF opposed the description of Gitmo as America's Battle Lab, or the contention that it was a place to experiment with detainees. It was duly noted and ignored. The army loved the phrase.

Two weeks later, Dunlavey followed up Custer's supportive report with a power grab. On September 23, 2002, ███████████, the CITF supervising agent at Gitmo, called me. "Mark, they're stealing our interrogation. Dunlavey is taking al-Qahtani before we get a chance."

Once the FBI was done with al-Qahtani, we were supposed to get the second pass, before JTF-170. But Dunlavey was a man enraged. He'd come into Gitmo thinking his success there would secure his legacy in the new war against terror. By this point, he'd found out he was being relieved of command early instead. He'd had very little success in intel collection, and reports of his strange behavior had been elevated up the chains of command. He was convinced his lack of success had something to do with the reputed Manchester Document training Al Qaeda operatives received. He needed to figure out a way to crush their resistance.

At the same time as Dunlavey was struggling, the CIA was claiming they were having enormous success with their enhanced interrogation techniques. The Agency was boasting about finding links between Al Qaeda and Iraq as well as intelligence that was used to disrupt attacks on the US. My sources were telling me the CIA wasn't having nearly the success they claimed. In fact, it turned out their intel on a stream of imminent attacks on the US was mostly successful at stressing out Americans and wasting law enforcement resources. But Dunlavey bought the CIA's claims hook, line, and sinker. The general wanted his third star—and he wasn't going to get it without an intel coup. He knew the CIA was using much tougher tactics during their interrogations. Turning up the pressure on al-Qahtani seemed like his best bet.

Dunlavey developed a plan that apparently involved grabbing al-Qahtani out of his cell, hooding him, and then driving around Guantanamo Bay to disorient him, stripping him to his underwear, and using an interrogator pretending to be an Egyptian. Detainees were well aware of the brutality of Egyptian interrogations.

I was already planning on flying down to Gitmo the next day, September 24, 2002. A delegation of senior government lawyers would be visiting on September 25. I wanted to make sure they got the real story about interrogation before Dunlavey's plans for al-Qahtani were approved.

CHAPTER 7

THE TORTURE ARCHITECTS

On September 24, 2002, I was on the early morning UC-35 Citation jet to Guantanamo. A group of distinguished visitors—DVs in military speak—was arriving the next day. These were some of the most important lawyers in the Global War on Terror, including Bush's lawyer, Alberto Gonzales; Vice President Dick Cheney's lawyer, David Addington; acting CIA general counsel John Rizzo; and Deputy Attorney General Michael Chertoff.

The trip was intended to give the group an update on the progress of the military commission cases. But this made no sense; CITF was the agency that was running the military commissions investigations. And CITF's executive headquarters wasn't in Guantanamo but Fort Belvoir. Instead of driving twenty minutes south from the Pentagon to get an update, they were flying to Cuba?

"Something stinks," I said to Mike Gelles. "And it's not on my shoes."

While I hadn't known the details of their trip at the time, it

seemed obvious this all-star legal team was flying down to Gitmo
to meet with Dunlavey. In counterintelligence, I learned to develop
indications and warnings about when an attack might occur. Because you never have all the facts, counterintelligence officials learn
to look at the whole field of circumstances and pinpoint anoma-
lies. In this case, the most senior lawyers in the new war on terror
were coming to Gitmo right in the middle of our struggle with
JTF-170 over how to interrogate al-Qahtani. It set off screaming
threat-warning alarms. I was afraid Dunlavey was going to sell the
lawyers a bill of goods—that torture was necessary and effective—
and, worse, that he would likely be successful. I was also developing
a new rule of thumb for the war on terror: where lawyers go, bad
things follow.

As the plane looped around the southern tip of Cuba, I thought,
*I just need to get in the room with these guys and explain to them how
an interrogation really works and persuade them why more enhanced
procedures won't.*

They weren't experts. Dunlavey was probably trying to pull the
wool over their eyes. His first step in taking unprecedentedly harsh
measures with al-Qahtani would be getting policy approval from
this team. But I was going to get my two cents in first. I couldn't let
Dunlavey's ridiculous plans win approval.

We bumped down on the runway that was already wavy with
heat. Thirty minutes later, the ferry pulled up on the east side of the
bay. An iguana was sunning itself down the pier. I looked north up
the hill, covered in grass that had browned over the summer. About
200 yards away sat the building originally designated for military
commissions. It hadn't seen much action in the nine months since
Gitmo had opened. If Dunlavey's plan got approved, we might as
well close it up.

· · ·

The CITF headquarters was just a ten-minute drive from the ferry landing. We had taken over the old daycare center, right in the middle of the residential section of the base. I walked in the door to bad news.

"Hey, Mark," said ███████. "How was the flight?"

"Not bad."

"Things are heating up."

"Already pretty hot," I said, grabbing a bottle of water.

"No. Dunlavey's been talking to Haynes." Jim Haynes was Rumsfeld's counsel at the Department of Defense. He was also part of the DVs delegation arriving the next day.

Jeff continued. "He's telling Haynes his interrogators are constrained. He wants to use more aggressive techniques." It was more complicated than that, though. Jim Haynes was also at the top of CITF's command chain. Dunlavey had the ear of the man we reported to at the Pentagon. Something stunk, all right.

I winced. *But it's OK,* I told myself. I had actual experience investigating terrorists. CITF and the FBI had discovered the identity of the twentieth hijacker. JTF-170 had nothing. Of course, this was probably part of the problem: Dunlavey was desperate to have anything to show for his miserable command at Gitmo.

The next day at 10:00 AM, I was standing just outside the Camp Delta command post, waiting to meet up with the lawyer delegation. In April we had finally gotten a new camp built for the swelling ranks of detainees and were able to close Camp X-Ray. Camp Delta was still a series of low-slung buildings surrounded by a maze of chain-link fences and concertina wire. Unlike the isolated X-Ray, Delta was plopped down right on the coast, where emerald water lapped up on rocks.

Fifteen minutes later, a small bus approached the post. As I walked out to greet the DVs, Dunlavey blew right past me. I caught up with the group and followed them through one of the new Camp Delta cellblocks. They were an upgrade from the crude conditions at Camp X-Ray, but hardly fancy. The blocks were built out of shipping containers welded together lengthwise to create a larger structure. A metal roof kept the rain out, but the cellblocks were otherwise open-air, their walls made out of a sturdy metal mesh. Each of the 6'x8' cells, barely big enough for one prisoner, had mesh doors with slots at waist height. The slots were just large enough for food trays to go in or hands to come out for cuffing. Inside their cells, about two dozen detainees in flaming-orange jumpsuits looked on as the lawyers silently walked down the narrow hallway in their dark suits. Some glared, others stared blankly.

The next stop for the DVs was an interrogation in another new facility. When they arrived, the detainee—a cooperative one who had been preselected—was talking with interrogators in a spare, beige-paneled room with a one-way mirror. On the other side, the lawyers stood in a darkened observation room. The whole thing was a show. It was the only way to make JTF-170's interrogation program look good.

Afterward, the group walked out to a waiting bus. I followed them to the door but was pulled aside by one of Dunlavey's assistants.

"Mark, you're not allowed on the bus." He looked a little uneasy.

"Why not?"

"Dunlavey thinks it would be inappropriate. He suggested you wait at the CITF headquarters to meet them following the JTF-170 briefing."

The group continued on to tour the medical facilities and visit the site of the future building for military commissions. I headed back to my task force headquarters.

While I waited, the senior lawyers sat around a table in a cramped conference room, listening to Dunlavey's pitch for additional interrogation techniques. "We'd like to take the Koran away from some detainees—hold it as incentive," suggested Dunlavey. It was just one of a long list of requests.

The other DVs in attendance were mostly silent, but Jim Haynes weighed in, saying Dunlavey should be able to implement additional forms of psychological pressure. Haynes opined, "JTF-170 should have the authority in place to make those calls per POTUS order. JTF-170 would have more freedom to command," said Haynes.

Though nothing was signed, the message that JTF-170 lawyer Diane Beaver took away was "Do what needs to be done." The lawyers implicitly green-lighted torture at Gitmo.

Meanwhile, I sat anxiously at my desk for an hour and a half before calling up Dunlavey's office.

"How long is this briefing going on?" I asked.

"It's over."

"OK. Good. Should I expect the DVs now?"

"No. They departed forty-five minutes ago."

"What?" I was incredulous. Dunlavey knew I would push back on his request in front of the lawyers. There was apparently no way he was going to let me in the room. I wanted to confront Dunlavey for icing me out, but I needed to get back up to Fort Belvoir that night. My pilots were telling me we had to leave right then to thread the needle between two potential hurricanes. Ultimately, there was nothing I could do at Gitmo to stop the spread of aggressive interrogations. All my best options at that point involved directly challenging JTF-170 through the official channels. I could do that just as well from Virginia.

The next week brought more lawyers. Specifically, our senior lawyer, Sam McCahon, and ██████████████, the ████████████ at the

CIA Counterterrorism Center.  I wasn't privy to the specifics ▮▮▮▮▮▮▮▮▮▮▮, although I did know ▮▮▮▮▮▮▮ had been abusing and rendering people around the world.

During the flight, Sam recalled Fredman leaning in toward him. "I know we disagree on the permissible techniques," said ▮▮▮▮▮ ▮▮▮, "but I have a memo from the attorney general saying they are legal and authorized."

"Really?" asked ▮▮▮. "I'd love to see that."

"I don't carry a copy around with me," said ▮▮▮▮▮▮.

"Maybe you should," said ▮▮▮ sarcastically.

It turned out that ▮▮▮▮▮▮ was not coming down to Gitmo to meet with ▮▮▮▮▮▮▮▮. He was meeting with Dunlavey's lawyer, Diane Beaver, and a half dozen others, among them psychologist ▮▮▮▮▮▮ and psychiatrist Paul Burney, the two behavioral scientists who had been drafted into JTF-170's pseudo-BSCT. They'd received training in SERE counterresistance techniques and had been developing plans to exploit al-Qahtani, but so far no one was able to define what "getting tougher" meant from a legal standpoint. I wasn't at the meeting, but it wasn't hard to guess what everyone hoped to get out of it. The delegation of lawyers that had met with Dunlavey the previous week talked about harsher interrogation on a policy level. But Dunlavey wasn't doing the interrogations. ▮▮▮▮ ▮▮▮ was meeting with the people who actually had to carry out Dunlavey's orders. He was there to offer ▮▮▮▮▮▮ advice on the legal nuts and bolts of what actually happened in an interrogation booth.

Among the other attendees was David Becker, a squirrely guy with the strange title of chief of the interrogation control element.

Becker was part of the DIA contingent who had begun staffing JTF-170's interrogation teams. Rounding out the main players were Dunlavey's intel chief Jerry Phifer, a skinny guy who never seemed well-liked, even by his own team, and Colonel Cummings, a broad-chested member of Dunlavey's staff whom I always figured for a stand-up guy.

When I found out about the meeting, I immediately sent one of my lawyers in to take detailed notes. "If someone burps," I said, "I want to know who."

Diane Beaver had called the meeting, but it was driven by Dunlavey's increasing frustration with his team's intel collection. He particularly wanted information that proved the link between Al Qaeda and Iraq.

Up to that point, the only such evidence had come from the head of a training camp director, Ibn Al-Shaykh al-Libi, who was captured in November 2001. He was initially interrogated by the FBI at Bagram Airfield in Afghanistan. During this period, the FBI agents had convinced al-Libi to give up some useful information on Richard Reid, the so-called Shoe Bomber, who in December 2001 tried to blow up Flight 63, en route from Paris to Miami, with plastic explosives packed into the hollowed-out bottom of his work boot.

But al-Libi didn't start talking about Al Qaeda in Iraq until a ███ officer marched into the FBI interrogation session and began yelling at him in Arabic: "You're going to ████! And while you're there, I'm going to find your mom and fuck her!"

████ and military police then grabbed al-Libi and carried him out of the room by his arms as the FBI agents watched. Al-Libi was strapped to a stretcher and thrown on an airplane to Egypt, where he was brutalized, eventually admitting there were high level connections between Al Qaeda and Iraq.

The Counter Resistance Strategy Meeting was called to order at 1:40 PM. Everyone present knew the CIA was already using enhanced interrogation techniques at black sites. They wanted ███ ███ to explain the legal nuances of these techniques. They wanted to know what they could get away with legally. However, ███ and Burney started out by mentioning that rapport-based techniques were likely more effective.

"Harsh techniques used on our service members have worked and will work on some," argued Phifer. "What about those?"

"Force is risky," said ███, "and may be ineffective due to the detainees' frame of reference. They are used to seeing much more barbaric treatment."

Having offered the truth about interrogation processes to a mostly uninterested room, ███ continued by advocating for the camp-wide program that could "manipulate all aspects of the detainees' environment to foster and complete compliance." This would include isolation and disrupting sleep patterns. The meeting's tone and content turned increasingly conspiratorial.

"We can't do sleep deprivation," said Colonel Cummings.

"Yes, we can," said Beaver, "with approval."

"We may need to curb the harsher operations while the ICRC [International Committee of the Red Cross] is around," warned Beaver. "It's better not to expose them to any controversial techniques. We must have the support of the DOD."

"We have had many reports from Bagram about sleep deprivation being used," said Becker.

"True," said Beaver, "but officially it is not happening. It's not being reported officially. The ICRC is a serious concern. They will be in and out, scrutinizing our operations, unless they are displeased and decided to protest and leave. That would draw a lot of negative attention."

███████ said the CIA was not held to the same standard as the military. "In the past, when the ICRC made a big deal about certain detainees, the DOD had moved them away from the attention of the ICRC." There was even a term for these disappearing people, "ghost detainees." They remained at the prison but were never seen again by the Red Cross.

The room fell briefly silent.

"The CIA has employed aggressive techniques on less than a handful of suspects since 9/11," said ███████. "Under the Torture Convention, torture has been prohibited by international law, but language of the statutes is written vaguely." He continued, "It's basically subject to perception. If the detainee dies, you're doing it wrong. So far, the techniques we have addressed have not proven to produce these types of results."

He added, "Everything in the BSCT white paper is legal from a civilian standpoint," referring to a document ███ and Burney had created listing techniques that seemed to go beyond the bounds of acceptable protocol.

"Any of the techniques that lie on the harshest end of the spectrum must be performed by a highly trained individual," advised ███████. "Medical personnel should be present to treat any possible accidents. The CIA operates without military intervention. When the CIA has wanted to use more aggressive techniques in the past, the FBI has pulled their personnel from theater. In those rare instances, aggressive techniques have proven very helpful."

"We'll need documentation to protect us," said Beaver.

"Yes," replied ███████. "If someone dies while aggressive techniques are being used, regardless of the cause of death, the backlash of attention would be severely detrimental. Everything must be approved and documented."

Becker advised that law enforcement agencies (LEAs) such as the FBI "will not participate in harsh sessions."

"There is no legal reason why LEA personnel cannot participate in these operations. Does SERE employ the wet towel technique?" asked Beaver.

"If a well-trained individual is used to perform this technique, it can feel like you're drowning," ████████ answered. "The lymphatic system will react as if you're suffocating, but your body will not cease to function. It's very effective to identify phobias and use them [i.e., insects, snakes, claustrophobia]. The level of resistance is directly related to a person's experience."

"In the BSCT paper it says something about 'imminent threat of death,'" Beaver noted.

"The threat of death is also subject to scrutiny and should be handled on a case-by-case basis," said ████████. "Mock executions don't work as well as friendly approaches, like letting someone write a letter home, or providing them with an extra book."

"I like the part about ambient noise," said Becker.

When the meeting adjourned at 2:50, Dunlavey, Phifer, Becker, and the behavioral scientists had policy cover from the senior interagency lawyer delegation that had visited the previous week. Now they had an argument for efficacy from the ████ counsel for the CIA Counterterrorism Center.

Back in Fort Belvoir, I got a phone call that ███████████ had provided the DOD torture architects with that high-level legal cover. They could counter any opposition from the CITF. I called my superiors at the Pentagon and asked them to do what they could to intercede. They listened, noted that they understood our position, and advised that they would report it up the chain. But ultimately they all worked for Jim Haynes, who was part of the problem. With the CIA touting their successes, no one took the issue on.

• • •

Meanwhile, ▇▇ and Burney had drafted a memo partially based on the SERE interrogation tactics they had learned at Fort Bragg. Some of the other techniques were made up. After all, Gitmo was the Battle Lab, a place for experimentation.

In academic fashion, ▇▇ and Burney divided detainee treatment into three categories. Category I techniques were described as "mildly adverse approaches"—such as threatening a detainee that he would be at Guantanamo forever. If, at the end of the session, the detainee was still uncooperative, interrogators could request Category II.

According to ▇▇ and Burney, Category II was for detainees "with intelligence relative to the security of the United States." It permitted, for example, hooding detainees, shackling them to the wall, and "dietary manipulation"—starving them for up to twelve hours.

The final level, Category III, was designed for detainees "that have evidenced resistance and are suspected of having significant information pertinent to national security." These detainees could be locked up with no human contact, including access to doctors. They could be dragged from those cells by soldiers yelling at them, shackled to the floor in a room, and interrogated for twenty hours a day, indefinitely. They could be left exposed in the cold "until such time as the detainee begins to shiver." Interrogators could pretend they were going to kill a detainee, even acting out the parts leading up to execution.

The doctors also recommended implementing a "controlled chaos" plan for the general population within the prison camp. Resistant detainees should be limited to four hours of sleep a day and deprived of "comfort items," such as sheets, blankets, mattresses, washcloths, toilet paper, Korans, and other religious items. Fans and generators could be used to create white noise.

"All aspects of the [detention] environment," the doctors recommended, "should enhance capture shock, dislocate expectations,
foster dependence, and support exploitation to the fullest extent
possible."

The paper included a disclaimer: "Experts in the field of interrogation indicate the most effective interrogation strategy is a
rapport-building approach." It also mentioned that physical pressures would not necessarily increase the flow of accurate information. These warnings only served to prove ████ and Burney knew
what they were doing was unscientific. In fact, they knew it was
wrong. And, finally, they were probably still not totally comfortable
with this document Dunlavey had asked them to produce. But instead of standing up to Dunlavey, they gave him exactly what he
wanted: medical cover to ratchet up pressure on al-Qahtani.

That same evening, JTF-170, the pseudo-BSCT unit, and interrogators from the Defense Intelligence Agency got busy. They
seized al-Qahtani from FBI control in the naval brig and transported him to Camp X-Ray. Initially X-Ray had been used because
there were no other alternatives. This time, it was an interrogation
tactic.

The camp had been crowded when he first arrived; now
al-Qahtani was alone. He sat at Camp X-Ray for days by himself.
Blinding lights kept him awake. Speakers were aimed at him, playing loud music such as Christina Aguilera's "Dirrty" over and over
again. At other times military dogs were brought into his cage to
bark and scare him.

The FBI allowed their personnel to observe al-Qahtani's interrogations, but if they saw abusive activity, they were to report
it to their unit chief. As long as there was no torture involved, the
FBI could participate. We pulled our people out. If they actually
witnessed—much less took part in—felonies and didn't take action,

it would put them in a very tight spot legally. In future cases, for example, defense attorneys could impeach them as witnesses. And if they did intervene—stop the action in progress and report it—it's likely the abusive interrogator(s) would have just been turned over to Dunlavey for referral. The general probably wouldn't have done squat. We also felt that our very presence might make it appear as if we sanctioned the actions.

A few days into the more aggressive treatment of al-Qahtani, psychiatrist Paul Burney sent an e-mail to psychologist Morgan Banks at Fort Bragg. It read, in part, "[P]ersons here at this operation are still interested in pursuing the potential use of more aversive interrogation tactics. . . . Were more aversive techniques approved for use in the future by appropriate people, the operation would like to have a few task force personnel specifically trained in various techniques."

"I do not envy you," Banks wrote back. He declined to provide any contact information for people who could train Gitmo personnel in even more abusive techniques than the SERE he had already trained them in. Banks told Burney that additional SERE techniques would probably not be useful. "The training that SERE instructors use is designed to simulate that of a foreign power [to] encourage resistance among students." Banks, who had eagerly arranged training for ▮▮▮▮ and Burney, seemed to be distancing himself from SERE tactics.

Whatever his real motivations, Banks was right. Al-Qahtani had originally been talkative. Toward the end of the FBI investigation, he began clamming up. But once the enhanced techniques began, al-Qahtani shut down completely. The FBI felt al-Qahtani's health was deteriorating. JTF-170 became convinced their techniques weren't enough to get additional intel out of al-Qahtani. On October 10, 2002, they moved him back to the navy brig.

Two days later, I learned General Rick Baccus, the commander of JTF-160, was going to be relieved of command, after just seven months. It wasn't much of a surprise, as Dunlavey hated Baccus. Just as Dunlavey accused me of being unpatriotic, he accused Baccus of "coddling detainees." As head of Military Police at Gitmo, Baccus not only treated prisoners well; he accommodated meal times for Ramadan, the month-long Islamic holiday when Muslims have to fast during daylight hours. For Dunlavey, this kind of respectful treatment by JTF-160 was making it harder for him to break down the detainees. With his intel coup still elusive and the clock ticking on his tenure, Dunlavey was doing anything possible to turn up the heat on the detainees.

The general may only have had a few weeks left, but he was still intent on removing all opposition to the psychologically abusive plans developed by his pseudo-BSCT. I kept empty boxes and a handcart in my office. Dunlavey had friends in high places. I wondered if I'd be fired next. In a way, getting booted might be a relief. While at Gitmo, I kept my demeanor professional. I said hello to Diane Beaver or Dave ███ if I passed them on the base. But it was getting harder. I hoped one day I'd see them, or Dunlavey, in an interrogation room, where I'd be reading them their Article 31B rights—the military equivalent of Miranda rights—before questioning.

Gitmo was also forcing me to expend energy protecting the people we wanted to see prosecuted. Al-Qahtani was likely the twentieth hijacker. He was fully prepared to fly a plane into the White House or Capitol. I didn't like him; I just didn't want our people breaking the law.

What's more, Guantanamo was just one aspect of CITF's mission. I still had people in Afghanistan flying helicopters and chasing bin Laden. Two hours after hearing the latest unsettling news from Gitmo, I'd be on the phone talking about a sensitive site exploitation, or an agent who had to hop on the back of a tank to get into a village.

On October 11, 2002, the day after al-Qahtani was moved back to the navy brig, Dunlavey requested authority for the Battle Lab to expand its ways of making him talk. Dunlavey had the legal cover provided by ▮▮▮▮▮▮ along with the medical authority offered by ▮▮▮ and Burney. He leveraged all this expert opinion to ask for official approval from the SOUTHCOM commander, General James T. Hill, to use the three categories of interrogation that his pseudo-BSCT had developed. In addition to the seventeen tactics described by Burney and ▮▮▮, there were two new ones: the use of phobias, and covering a detainee's face with a wet towel and dripping water on it to create the sense of suffocation—what some people call waterboarding or water treatment. These additional tactics may have appeared as a result of the CIA counsel ▮▮▮▮▮▮▮▮ recommendations at the October 2 meeting.

Accompanying Dunlavey's official request was a cover memo by Diane Beaver bluntly stating, "the proposed strategies do not violate applicable federal law."

Beaver had written this far-reaching memorandum with the limited legal resources available at Guantanamo. Though two weeks earlier she had met with some of the most powerful lawyers in the government, they had only offered policy cover. To justify the specific techniques the pseudo-BSCT had developed, she was now forced to rely on her own admittedly incomplete knowledge of the applicable laws. Beaver cobbled together some additional information from the Internet, such as it was in Gitmo in 2002. In a sense, this lack of complete access to precedents and huge bodies of law may have made the process easier. Beaver didn't know anything about international law, so she primarily steered clear of those issues. She figured someone further up the chain of command would have a better understanding of the subject matter, anyway. And the president had already said the Geneva Conventions didn't apply to these detainees, so she didn't challenge that. Beaver focused on American law, but even there she might have lost her critical edge.

Dunlavey was under huge pressure to get intel—and it came right down the chain of command to Beaver. She knew the general wanted an opinion in favor of these enhanced interrogation techniques. Like so many other people, Beaver also felt that national security was at risk if the United States couldn't figure out a way to get information from detained terrorists. Squelching the terrorist threat was also a personal mission to her; Beaver had been in the Pentagon on 9/11 when the plane hit. Moreover, the most popular TV show at Gitmo that year, *24*, suggested torturing terrorists was the kind of thing heroic and attractive people do to save lives. So it's possible that all these factors were weighing on Beaver's mind as she compared each of the techniques Dunlavey had requested against the Eighth Amendment's ban on cruel and unusual punishment. In the end she found the amendment did not ban any tactic "applied in a good faith effort and not maliciously and sadistically for the very purpose of causing harm."

In a few pages, Beaver wiped away all of the many legal safeguards against torture. But just in case some interrogation techniques violated the uniform code of military justice, Beaver had one more legal innovation: granting interrogators "advance immunity" from punishment for these crimes.

When the head of SOUTHCOM, General Hill, received the request, he fully endorsed the Category I and II techniques ███ and Burney had developed, although he was unsure about the legality of the Category III measures. His lawyers, and those at the army, navy, air force, and marines, had plenty of additional concerns about the audacious document. In the end, the most senior lawyers for each of the four military services were on record opposing JTF-170's "counter-resistance strategies."

Even when Dunlavey's request made it up to the chairman of the Joint Chiefs of Staff, the counsel to the chairman, Navy Captain Jane Dalton, found Beaver's legal analysis "woefully inadequate" and believed there were "significant, significant concerns" with the Category II and III techniques. But with the strongly worded endorsement from Hill, Dalton was unwilling to unilaterally oppose the request. Instead she began a legal review and set up a video conference with Gitmo, DIA, and SOUTHCOM.

That was as far as Dalton got. The chairman of the Joint Chiefs of Staff, General Richard Myers, ordered her to stop the review. The draft memos Dalton's staff had begun writing stated: "We do not believe the proposed plan to be legally sufficient." That's lawyer talk for *illegal*. But no one ever saw the memos.

CHAPTER 8

HONOR BOUND TO DEFEND FREEDOM

I first met the incoming commander of the new unified Joint Task Force Guantanamo (JTF-GTMO), General Geoffrey Miller, at 12:30 PM on October 28, 2002. Miller was an artillery officer with no background in intel who had previously served as the army's deputy chief of staff for personal and installation management. Artillery guys are trained to hold ground and repeatedly pound a target with kinetic energy to achieve an objective. It was a very different culture from the intel world, but we were still excited to have a regular general taking over at Guantanamo. Not only had Dunlavey been pursuing abusive interrogation tactics but his bizarre behavior was undermining discipline. Maybe Miller could provide the levelheaded leadership so lacking during Dunlavey's tenure. To get our relationship off on the right foot, Britt Mallow and I invited Miller down to the glamorous CITF headquarters to share all the intel and interrogation expertise Dunlavey had ignored.

First appearances don't necessarily mean much, but I couldn't help noticing when Miller walked in the door he had an extraordinarily rigid posture, even for a career military officer. We shook hands as he walked into the office, and then I led him over to the conference room. His posture, I would soon find out, wasn't the only thing unyielding about the man. During the two hours we spent together, Miller made it clear that his primary objective was to unify and integrate the detention and intelligence operations at Guantanamo. He told us he'd learned at his Pentagon pre-briefings that CITF was constantly interfering with the Gitmo intelligence-collection mission. He wanted our function to be subordinate to him, rather than having a separate reporting chain of command. In fact, he wanted complete control of everything pertaining to detainees at Guantanamo.

Miller also had a curious verbal tick—ending his sentences in "hoo-ah." For example, "CITF needs to be a team player, hoo-ah." Was he just being gung-ho? Maybe, but the way he said "hoo-ah" made me think of small-arms fire. The more I listened to him, the more I found myself worrying that Guantanamo was going to be led not by a voice of reason but by its exact opposite—a guy who insisted on doing things his own way and damn the results. Sort of like the general who was just departing—but a more competent hard-ass.

After Miller left, I sat back down in my seat, deflated. The phone rang. The army assistant chief of staff for intelligence, Terry Ford, was on the line to let me know the Guantanamo request for aggressive interrogation techniques had already been forwarded to the Joint Chiefs of Staff. This was unusually fast—and not hard to figure out. Just like Dunlavey, Miller could bypass the chain of command and directly contact the secretary of defense. Miller wanted the authorities for advanced interrogations in place for his arrival, and Rumsfeld's office was going to get it for him. Miller wasn't coming to Gitmo to fix Dunlavey's mess. He was being brought in to execute the strategy that Dunlavey began.

On November 4, 2002, Miller officially became JTF-GTMO's first commander. He started his term with a new motto: "Honor bound to defend freedom."

When soldiers on base saluted each other, one would say: "Honor bound!"

The other would respond: "Defend freedom!"

Signs adorned with the new logo went up everywhere, on the base entrances and in the lobbies of buildings. It was painted, one letter at a time, on the cement barriers outside the prison camp fences.

Miller also immediately established his totalitarian management style, one that seemed to mesh well with Rumsfeld's. He had little patience for anything that didn't comport with the manner in which he wanted to execute his mission. Miller's approach to interrogation was just as nuanced. He even had a tag line for how to deal with detainees: "We've got to show them that we have more teeth than they have ass, hoo-ah!"

Miller's forceful style did win him some adherents. Psychologist Larry James—███ former mentor who had arranged for him to get SERE training—couldn't say enough good things about Miller. James described Miller as "the kind of commander you wanted to be around—a soldier's soldier, all business and no bullshit."

After initially just advising ███, James joined Miller's pseudo-BSCT and took over running it. Once at Gitmo, he told Miller the Army Field Manual FM 34-52 "Intelligence Interrogation" wasn't the best guidance on the subject. "[W]hat I can bring to the table, sir, is my knowledge of psychology and how to best get people to talk. There are better ways, more effective ways, to get this intel." James viewed Gitmo as a career opportunity to psychologically exploit detained prisoners. In exchange, Miller told him to advise the interrogators on tactics, even though James had no interrogation experience himself.

James wasted no time. "Everything about General Miller screamed 'action,'" he later wrote in *Fixing Hell*. "You felt like you should always be doing something productive, getting things done, not standing around like a slack-ass. So with that in mind, I didn't waste any time getting to my main task at Gitmo—improving the way we interrogated prisoners."

With authority granted to utilize additional interrogation tactics, some of them untested, James was in the right place. Detainees at Gitmo would become part of an experiment to test psychological theories and control human behavior in custodial conditions. JTF-GTMO called their new psychologist-driven activities Behavior Management Plans. One plan called for immediate thirty-day isolation for detainees upon arrival at Gitmo. Their objective was, before any other tactics were used, to create dread and make the detainees totally dependent on the interrogators. The pseudo-BSCT was practicing the theory of "learned helplessness, but they renamed it "demonstrated omnipotence."

CITF's treatment didn't improve either. We retained our separate chain of command, which made us the loose cannon on Miller's deck—the one unit he didn't have total control over. It was obvious that our freedom irked him to no end. It was equally obvious that he had no time or patience for other perspectives on how to handle interrogations. We tried to get Mike Gelles—who had more interrogation consultation experience than everyone on the pseudo-BSCT combined—in to speak with Miller. But the new commander was much less accessible than Dunlavey. He required an appointment in advance, as well as a briefing package, with bullets on what was going to be discussed for his staff to analyze in advance. Miller told CITF he only believed in "by-the-numbers staffing" and wasn't going to accept any appointments for discussions. The meeting with Gelles never even happened.

Eight days after he arrived, Miller used the authority he'd been given and requested final approval for an enhanced interrogation plan for al-Qahtani. At this point, support for psychologically harsh interrogation at Gitmo had been voiced in some form or another by top lawyers in the administration, the military, and the CIA. Miller's team also had support for efficacy of the procedures as well as medical cover from Morgan Banks. So why did Dunlavey and then Miller keep asking for additional approval? First, they were working in a command-and-control structure; a novel undertaking in the army simply means filling out lots of paperwork. But there was also something darker than bureaucratic protocol at work: the generals knew they were breaking the law. In fact, all the way up the chain of command, the numerous legal reviews and secret memos were not just an exercise in ass covering but a kind of guilty gesture.

On November 14, ███████████████ received an e-mail from Diane Beaver. Beaver advised it was her "understanding" that the National Security Counsel had weighed in and stated that the intelligence from al-Qahtani was an "utmost matter of national security," adding, "We are driving forward with the support of SOUTHCOM." The apparent support of the National Security Counsel and SOUTHCOM was finally enough to stop JTF-GTMO's obsessive approval seeking. Miller planned to begin interrogating al-Qahtani at midnight on November 15, 2002.

Our last option to prevent these abusive practices at Gitmo was to go on the offensive with Miller. Britt Mallow and I crafted an e-mail that would go straight to Miller. Our message needed to be direct yet not threatening. We tried to reach him on his responsibilities as a leader, mentioning that the use of such techniques could "open any military member up for potential criminal charges." We thought if we could impress upon Miller that there might be consequences for his decision to use more abusive techniques on al-Qahtani, he might pause and research the matter more thoroughly. After all, he had just assumed command there. We thought we might convince him he was going down a path, or being led down a path, that had unintended outcomes.

We also wanted to leave Miller a way out, so it would be his decision, not something forced upon him. We proposed the JTF-GTMO and CITF create a "joint working group," where JTF-GTMO, CITF, FBI, and CIA could all participate in the development of a detailed interrogation plan for al-Qahtani. At a minimum, we hoped we could buy more time so we could engage the issue.

We wordsmithed the e-mail a few times, going back and forth about the tone and wanting to be indirectly direct. But even if we got the tone correct, the truth is, in the command-and-control structure of the military, colonels don't write letters like this to major generals. Finally, Britt sat at his desk, with me looking over his shoulder, staring at the unsent e-mail.

"Should I send it?" he asked.

"Go for it!"

"Are you sure?"

"Hit SEND, Britt."

He took a deep breath and hit the SEND button. The moment his finger left the keyboard I yelled, "No, I was just kidding! Don't send it!" I burst out laughing. So did Britt, once the horror left his face.

For once, our efforts paid off. Al-Qahtani's interrogation did not commence at midnight. Miller had blinked. Maybe he was coming around.

The first sign that our hopes were misplaced came just three days later. On November 18, 2002, JTF-GTMO implemented what they called a Rewards and Penalties program that wasn't aimed just at al-Qahtani but was Gitmo-wide. If interrogators felt the detainees were uncooperative or untruthful, they would order them into isolation cells, where they could choose to blast the air-conditioning or leave the detainees baking in the tropical heat. These tactics were part of ███ and Burney's descriptions of creating "controlled chaos" throughout the camp.

If there was any doubt Miller was still hell-bent on using the EITs at Gitmo, it disappeared during a November 21 senior-level secure video teleconference. Miller used the meeting to pitch his program to the Pentagon. The general said his staff felt the EITs were necessary to obtain the intelligence that was essential to our national security.

Miller then made a series of questionable claims. First, he said his pseudo-BSCT was on board. From the discussions he'd had with the psychologist ███ and psychiatrist Burney, Mike Gelles wasn't sure this was true. In fact, he had become convinced these key members of Miller's pseudo-BSCT knew the EITs were wrong and ineffective—they just couldn't stand up to their general. Miller also cited the positive legal opinion from his own staff judge advocate. He failed to mention that every other lawyer who reviewed Diane Beaver's October cover letter felt her legal reasoning was way off base. Finally, Miller claimed the FBI supported his interrogation plan for al-Qahtani. This was an outright lie, but Miller was an artillery officer—relentlessly pounding to achieve his objective.

To push back against Miller's arguments, we had Mike Gelles patched in from Guantanamo and ███████ and Sam McCahon at the Pentagon, along with the FBI Guantanamo unit

chief. I watched from the CITF conference room with my senior staff. We put everything on the line. We made clear that the
EITs were illegal, immoral, ineffective, and unconstitutional. Our
orders—from the president—were to treat detainees humanely. It
was the CITF on one side of the issue and the new field general
on the other. Miller, with less than a month in place as the JTF-
GTMO commander, didn't have a clue what an effective interrogation technique might be. He just opposed anything that wasn't
under his direct command and control. He was dead set on using
SERE in interrogations, and he didn't care what anybody else said.

After the meeting, the FBI was incensed Miller had lied about
their support of the plan, but they were also concerned that if they
made a stink about it, they could be asked to leave Gitmo alto-
gether, potentially missing out on intel. However, ███████████, an
FBI agent with the Behavioral Analysis Unit, ███████████████
██
███████████████████████████████. The FBI counsel responded
that, absent human rights violations, "such as physical torture, rape,
starvation and murder," the military's authority was not the FBI's
concern. The techniques were "apparently lawful" for the military.
However, FBI agents should not be "involved in" such interrogations. If FBI agents were uncomfortable in such a situation, they
should leave.

Unsatisfied with the response, Neer sent official correspondence to FBI headquarters with concerns that FBI personnel were
witnessing sleep deprivation, duct tape on detainees' mouths, loud
music, bright lights, and growling dogs being used in JTF-GTMO's
interrogations, putting FBI personnel in a tenuous situation. That
official correspondence was never responded to.

After the recent stay of al-Qahtani's enhanced interrogation, I
had felt a ray of hope. Now I could feel the darkness encroaching.

We kept advocating for proven techniques. Few people ever directly disputed our arguments, but the treatment of detainees kept getting harsher. The way everything at Gitmo was tracking, I could see congressional committee hearings on the horizon. I began to worry not just about preventing detainee abuse but protecting my staff and myself. When we registered concerns, I sent messages to other CITF staff, as well as to Ralph Blincoe at NCIS headquarters. "Ralph: Please ensure you save a copy of this. . . . I may need it in the future. I'll keep you posted."

By now I had realized whoever was behind this push to torture was powerful. I began e-mailing key documents to trusted friends and told them to save them. If things went sideways, I could be relieved of command and denied access to my office and e-mails. I needed to stash documentary evidence of everyone's actions at Guantanamo at safe locations. I felt like I was undercover again, working within a criminal enterprise planning a heist.

I also told our legal counsel, Sam, to take notes and document every contact he had with the DOD Office of General Counsel. The mission to bring bad guys to justice was being subverted by forces beyond my level. I would add it to my list of failures. I had to protect the CITF personnel. I had to fulfill my promise to Donald Ryder to protect my people.

Al-Qahtani's fate was sealed on November 27, 2002, when Department of Defense lawyer Jim Haynes signed an action memo for Donald Rumsfeld on the counterresistance techniques, with the memos from Phifer, Beaver, Dunlavey, and Hill attached.

Five days later, Secretary Rumsfeld signed the request that Dunlavey had originally initiated, authorizing eighteen of the interrogation techniques that emanated from Guantanamo. In reference to the request for forcing detainees to stand in stress positions for four hours at a time, Rumsfeld added a handwritten note: "However, I stand for 8–10 hours a day. Why is standing limited to 4 hours?"

The CITF had been cut out of any decision making, but we still had access to an electronic interrogation log recording al-Qahtani's treatment. At the earlier meetings, ███████████████████ ███████████████████████ So I had our analyst send the logbook's entries up to me every day. Miller's team had no idea we had access to them.

██
██████████████████
██
██
██
██
██████████████████████████████
██
██
██
██
███████████████████
██
██
████████████████████████████

Al-Qahtani's extreme reaction to the female interrogator was calculated. The interrogators knew that many of the detainees were brought up in a culture where women dressed very modestly. In some cases, they may have grown up never seeing a women in public without her whole body covered. Certainly, open sexuality or nudity were shocking taboos. For Americans and Europeans, this taboo might only be imaginable if they inserted their cousins or siblings in the role of female interrogators, and imagined them stripping and rubbing up against them.

Reading the logbook, it was striking to me how, as with so many other things, JTF-GTMO's use of females was the polar opposite of CITF and NCIS's. In fact, when I put together my interrogation team for Guantanamo, I purposefully selected more men than women. Given strict Arab Muslims' very different attitudes toward sexuality and women—how they dress, behave, etc.—I thought I would be setting up even the most experienced female interrogators to fail. I was wrong. It turned out that a number of women were among our most successful, but it was because they acted professional, not through sexual exploitation.

My best guess on this unexpected twist is that, because most Middle Eastern men revere their mothers, these females became a sort of surrogate. I have no research to validate this, but CITF female interrogators seemed to listen better, have more sympathy, and didn't make the detainees uncomfortable by getting too close. Whatever the case, it was a lot more effective than just trying to freak out detainees with women's bodies.

[redacted]

Medical professionals—including ▮▮▮▮▮ and Paul Burney— were direct participants in this treatment. Begrudgingly at times, they had helped develop, recommend, and implement practices that were cruel, inhumane, and degrading. ▮▮▮ was actually in the room giving interrogators advice. He would tell interrogators to spin al-Qahtani around in a chair so he could not focus his eyes on an object. He would also assess al-Qahtani to determine if his abuse could continue.

Burney was also present for parts of al-Qahtani's interrogation, including when he was stripped, when he was forcibly groomed, when a female interrogator invaded his personal space, when he was threatened with a military working dog, and when he was treated like an animal—forced to wear a leash or act like a dog. They were testing Seligman's theory on humans. And in the most twisted sense, they were successful.

[redacted]

Reading the logbooks on a daily basis in my office at Fort Belvoir, I became angry at myself for feeling sympathy for a terrorist as well as frustrated by my inability to stop the torture and by the dwindling options in front of me. Dave Brant had authorized me to pull the NCIS agents from the CITF if I saw the situation deteriorate to an untenable level. However, if we withdrew from the CITF, we wouldn't have access to the torture logs.

I decided to get in touch with John Pistole, the FBI's assistant director for counterterrorism, to try to see if the FBI could help. They couldn't. While the FBI didn't agree with the aggressive techniques, their official position was that it was a DOD matter and out of their hands.

Then I called Ralph Blincoe to discuss my reflections about Gitmo and the risks I associated with NCIS being involved in any way with interrogations. Ralph was not only my reporting senior within NCIS but one of my closest friends. Over the many years, when we'd asked each other for support, the response was either "Anything for you, buddy" or "As long as it's not a felony!" But there was little Ralph could do at that point. He encouraged me to hang in there, just like a contact agent does with an undercover agent.

By that point, EITs were already established practice in the CIA. That summer, Abu Zubaydah had served as their test case. Dunlavey was essentially using al-Qahtani as a test case for harsh interrogation of detainees within the DOD. But even with all the support he'd received up to that point, it would be easier to move forward with the Category III tactics on al-Qahtani if there was evidence within the military that such techniques were already in use. So in order to bolster the efficacy arguments for SERE techniques at Guantanamo, CENTCOM sent a list of interrogation techniques they had been using at the Bagram collection point in Afghanistan. The list was meant to portray tactics at Gitmo as already widespread in use, as well as necessary and effective.

They had it backward, though. The techniques being used by the CENTCOM Special Mission Unit in Afghanistan were actually adopted when SMU personnel from Afghanistan had visited Guantanamo in October. The SMU came to Gitmo immediately following JTF-170's SERE training at Fort Bragg and ██████████ ████████████████████. At the Battle Lab, the Afghanistan-based task force learned what techniques were going to be used by interrogators at Gitmo.

Without authorization, the SMU had gone back to Afghanistan and proposed the use of strip searches for degradation purposes, sensory deprivation, dogs, and environmental manipulation through "cold, heat, wet, discomfort, etc." With their training received at Guantanamo, the SMU had also advocated for "psychological/physical stress" and "psychological deception leading to learned helplessness and increased compliance." But, though they learned the techniques at Gitmo, the interrogators in Afghanistan had more fully adopted the untested SERE tactics first.

Seligman's theory was spreading in a sort of torture Ponzi scheme. Interrogation teams at both Guantanamo and Bagram Airfield were each using the other's actions to justify the use of SERE tactics. Both sides were promising a high return on investment with little risk.

There was, however, enormous risk. These abuses sometimes became fatal. In late November 2002, an Afghan named Gul Rahman died of exposure while in CIA custody in Kabul after being left chained to a wall in nearly freezing temperature overnight. A few weeks later, in early December, a twenty-two-year-old taxi driver, known only by the name Dilawar, and the brother of a Taliban leader, Mullah Habibullah, had been killed in the custody of their military captors in Bagram. Both had severe blunt-force trauma on the back of their legs from repeated blows from US soldiers while in custody. Even after military medical examiners had ruled the two deaths homicides and autopsies had confirmed that the repeated blows to the legs had caused both men's hearts to cease functioning, US military general officers were telling the media there were no indications of abuse by soldiers.

We were killing detainees in Afghanistan. I was concerned we would kill al-Qahtani at Gitmo as well.

CHAPTER 9

PROTECT YOUR CLIENT

By December 2002 Dave Brant had had enough and decided to see what he could do personally with the echelon of military lawyers. He contacted Alberto Mora, the navy general counsel.

"I'm receiving reports of detainee abuse at Gitmo," Dave said. "Do you want to hear more?" Dave knew the Pentagon landscape well. This wasn't technically a navy issue. Mora didn't have to listen. And once he knew what was going on, he could be found culpable if he chose to ignore it. Dave wanted to give Mora a way out. But Mora asked for the details.

███
███
███
████████████████

Brant's call piqued Mora's interest, so the next day, Ralph Blincoe, Mike Gelles, and I went to see the top navy lawyer in his Pentagon office. The distinguished-looking Mora showed us back past his large mahogany desk to a tiny conference room that was soon crammed with some of the top lawyers in the marines and navy.

We had brought the logs of al-Qahtani's abuse, as well as Diane Beaver's memos. As I got into her assertions, I saw heads shaking and eyebrows rise. They thought it was the result of renegade low-level amateurs. Who tries to get actionable intelligence by having a detainee wear women's underwear? Gelles then described the coercive psychological exploitation that was the basis of the EIT program. Mora and the other lawyers in the room sat silently. I wondered what would come next. I had grown so used to everyone saying, "I agree with you, but not at the cost of my job."

Instead Mora cut to the chase: "We've got to do something about this. This is the worst piece of legalese I've ever seen."

He turned to me. "Did you explain to them what your background is? That this sort of work is what you've been doing for years?"

"Mr. Mora, I've been running this task force since its inception—they know. I've tried to explain this. I just have been unsuccessful in getting anyone to take any action. No one disagrees with me, but no one will do anything because Rumsfeld says you can do this."

First, Mora asked me to go down to Gitmo one more time and see if I could reason with Miller. I understood the implication. If Mora actually pursued this case, he'd practically be falling on his sword. He was appointed by President Bush and slotted to likely become either general counsel to the CIA or general counsel to the NSA. He might be giving all that up to back me.

"You got it," I said.

On December 19, 2002, Mora met with Army General Counsel Steven Morello and Army Deputy General Counsel Tom Taylor.

He thought these issues must have been misunderstood or not fully communicated.

Morello told him otherwise and showed him the chain of documents, from Dunlavey's original request through SOUTHCOM to the action memo from DOD General Counsel Jim Haynes authorizing the SERE tactics, which Rumsfeld had signed.

"Haynes must not have fully read that," said Mora.

"We tried to stop it," said Morello. "We were told not to question the decision."

In the military, such a response from higher authority is generally enough to shut down a query, but Mora had no intention of letting the chain of command stop him.

Following his meeting with Morello, Mora reviewed the December 2 request for enhanced techniques. Because the request had gone up the army chain of command, not the navy one, it had never crossed Mora's desk previously. Mora later wrote a letter to the navy inspector general, in which he wrote, "I regarded the memo as a wholly inadequate analysis of the law and a poor treatment of this difficult and highly sensitive issue." Even if the techniques didn't meet some high-bar definition of torture, he added, they were clearly illegal as cruel and inhuman treatment.

On December 20 Mora went to see Jim Haynes to convey his concerns and objections. Mora told Haynes that NCIS had advised him of Guantanamo detainee interrogation abuses and that NCIS considered abuses to be unlawful and contrary to American values. Mora told Haynes the techniques authorized in Rumsfeld's memo could rise to the level of torture.

"I have to disagree," replied Haynes.

Mora replied that Beaver's legal brief justifying the interrogation tactics was "an incompetent product of legal analysis" and urged Haynes not to rely on it.

Mora also brought to Haynes's attention Rumsfeld's handwritten note about how standing for more than four hours seemed appropriate. Mora argued such a comment could be interpreted as "a coded message" to interrogators "that they should not feel bound by the limits set in the memo but consider themselves authorized to do what was necessary to obtain the necessary information." It could open up Rumsfeld to be called as a witness at trials before military commissions. Once there, defense lawyers could ask the secretary of defense, under oath, to describe the abusive tactics he had approved to be used on their clients. It would be, at best, a horrible embarrassment for the administration.

Mora walked out of Haynes's office confident he had made his point. It had been a nasty mix-up, but with all the facts now in front of Haynes, Mora couldn't imagine the Pentagon lawyer wouldn't do his job. Haynes would seek to correct the mistakes and suspend the authority to apply the EITs within the defense department. Pleased that the future at Gitmo would at least be better than the past, Mora flew to Miami to spend Christmas with his family.

• • •

██
██
██
██
██
██
███████████████████████

Day after day, it had become clear that the SERE techniques were still not working, so two navy SERE instructors, John Rankin and Christopher Ross, flew to Guantanamo to train JTF-GTMO in yet more exploitation techniques. Neither of the instructors had any experience relevant to interrogations. Nonetheless, they taught the questioners at Gitmo how to apply physical pressures, such as insult slaps, walling, and stress positions. They also included the psychological pressures from Biderman's principles—the ones Chinese and North Korean communists had used to elicit false confessions.

The techniques apparently worked. ████████████████████
██

██████████ This was in keeping with Albert Biderman's 1957 observation that the real psychological stressors occur when the exploited person believes he is bringing the torture on himself. Following their visit with SERE psychologist Morgan Banks at Fort Bragg, Burney and ████ had described such techniques as "extremely effective," but "Effective at what?" remained the question.

██
██
██
██
██

al-Qahtani was no more forthcoming with useful intel. Rather than turn him into a babbling chatterbox of Al Qaeda secrets, the SERE approaches served only to harden al-Qahtani's resistance.

There was one significant effect, though, of all this concentrated detainee abuse: The odds of us ever bringing al-Qahtani to trial in the courtroom being built for military hearings were naught. His abuse at the hands of government interrogators could be used as discoverable material in any defense of him, or in a case against interrogators, psychologists, or the general who ordered it.

On January 6, Brant informed Alberto Mora that detainee abuse was continuing and that Rumsfeld's authorization remained in effect. Clearly, Haynes hadn't urged Rumsfeld to revoke the authorization for EITs, but Haynes had also underestimated the man who had encouraged him to do so. Mora's mother had fled Nazi Hungary in 1941. Her family moved to Boston, where she met Mora's dad, and Alberto was born in 1951. The family moved to Cuba, where they lived for eight years until they fled the Castro revolution. Twice in as many decades, his family had been forced to flee political violence and repression. With a history like that, Mora wasn't inclined to back down in the face of a Pentagon lawyer, even a highly placed one.

Two days after Dave Brant alerted him to the continued detainee abuse, Alberto Mora relaunched his one-person crusade, meeting with Jaymie Duran, a special assistant to both Rumsfeld and Deputy Secretary of Defense Paul Wolfowitz. Mora explained to Duran that the abuses were contrary to American values and would likely have severe policy repercussions. Public support for the Global War on Terror would diminish. International condemnation was assured. Duran expressed serious concern and asked to be kept informed.

On January 9, Mora confronted Haynes again. "Protect your

client!" he warned. Even if Haynes didn't care about torture, he had a responsibility to end interrogation policies that could threaten Rumsfeld's tenure. If Rumsfeld fell, then even the presidency might be damaged.

A few days afterward, I flew down to Gitmo for the meeting with Miller that I'd promised Mora. Miller's office was up a long, winding hill overlooking the base in a large building that used to run signal intel operations in the mid twentieth century. I made my case, while Miller listened with his lips jutting forward. When I was done, he quickly answered: "If you want to be on the team, you got to wear the same jersey, hoo-ah."

"I'm not on your team," I said. "I've got a different chain of command. And we're not going to concur with you or approve this. We simply disagree with the course of action that you've taken."

He didn't like that answer and threatened to deny me access to the intel his team was gathering. I wasn't going to lose any sleep over that. He clearly had no idea I was reading the interrogation logs.

On January 16, after I had briefed Mora on my meeting with Miller, he drafted a memo to Jim Haynes, stating he would officially document the legal view that the approved techniques were unlawful. In the buttoned-up Pentagon legal universe, this was the equivalent of the nuclear option. Mora's memo would document the legal opinion of a senior at the Office of General Counsel that the EITs were clearly cruel and likely torture. This wasn't something that could be easily ignored at the top levels of the Pentagon. Mora had the courage and character to say, "Hell no!"

Mora also had Haynes backed into a corner, or so it seemed. Just as Dunlavey and Miller were chasing their third stars, so Haynes wanted to be appointed as a federal judge. A written legal opinion like this from Mora could derail his aspirations. To forestall a black mark like that, Haynes had Rumsfeld suspend the EITs immediately, but once again, the relief was only temporary.

As soon as he suspended the program, Rumsfeld started looking for another way to create legal cover so he could reinstate it. He decided to appoint a "working group" to investigate Mora's claims, and those of other lawyers, that the interrogation tactics in question constituted cruel, abusive behavior—if not outright torture. Inside the Beltway, "working groups" are famous for providing cover for the person who appoints them, and this one was no exception. The whole process was a whitewash. The working group included Dave Becker, one of the people who designed the program at Gitmo, and Richard Shiffrin, the lawyer who was the first person in the Department of Defense's Office of Legal Counsel (OLC) to ask for information about SERE tactics.

To be sure, senior military lawyers opposed to the proposed interrogations tactics were given free license to weigh in against them. Among other issues, they pointed out that sanctioning these techniques would have a negative effect on the treatment of US military personnel captured as POWs and would adversely affect both human collection efforts and foreign-enemy force surrenders. During WWII, for example, many German troops surrendered to Americans rather than Russians, because they thought they'd get better treatment. Having an enemy fight to the death, rather than surrender, places troops at greater risk. It also negates intel collection from captured enemies, because the number of soldiers captured is very few.

But basically that was all cover for a predetermined outcome. Rumsfeld's working group ignored all the Department of Defense lawyers, relying instead on the White House Office of Legal Counsel arguments authored by John Yoo, which held that only serious physical injury, such as organ failure, the impairment of bodily functions, or death were prohibited.

Captain Jane Dalton, lawyer for the chairman of the Joint Chiefs of Staff, was "very angry" that the working group would use the OLC legal analysis rather than the Pentagon's legal interpretation. The group, she said, had been "geared toward a particular conclusion."

When Mora saw a draft version of the report, he said it contained "profound mistakes in its legal analysis, in large measure because of its reliance on the flawed OLC memo." Mora's advice to Haynes: Put the flawed report "in a drawer and never [let it] see the light of day."

This time, Mora believed his advice really had been taken, because he never saw a final version. In fact, the report approving (or "reapproving," to be more exact) torture techniques was stealthily finalized on April 4, 2003, but with one significant change: the word "SERE," which had been on the other drafts, was omitted. Maybe that was just a last-minute typographical error, but all subsequent actions suggest another explanation: Rumsfeld was intent on treating detainees harshly, and Haynes and others were doing everything they could to give the secretary of defense what he wanted. Omitting "SERE" wouldn't change a damn thing, but it might help the approval fly under the radar. And it did just that.

CHAPTER 10

THE AMERICAN AZKABAN

Which came first, the chicken or the egg? Who knows? But as this whole working-group drama was playing out to what I'm convinced was a predetermined end, Geoffrey Miller was already planning to expand the Battle Lab's experiments. On January 16, 2003, as we were flying back from our unsuccessful meeting with him, Miller submitted a request to administer the EIT program developed for al-Qahtani on another detainee.

Mohamedou Ould Slahi had turned himself in ▮▮▮▮▮▮ ▮▮▮ authorities in November 2001 for questioning with regard to the turn-of-the-century Millennium Plot, a series of unsuccessful al-Qaeda attacks planned for around the end of 1999 and early 2000. The evidence was circumstantial: Slahi had traveled briefly to Afghanistan just before the Soviets departed, ready to fight for Al Qaeda, and he had been living in Montreal in late 2000, where he attended the same mosque as Ahmed Ressam, who would ultimately be convicted of plotting to attack Los Angeles International

Airport with explosives in late December 1999. ██████████ officials found nothing to suggest Slahi had aided Ressam, but they nonetheless passed him off to the CIA, which promptly rendered Slahi ████████████████████████████████████
██. Slahi was held there for eight months, during which time he gave no credible intel or incriminating evidence. Figuring he was a dead end, the CIA turned Slahi over to US military custody in Afghanistan.

Slahi's story—abducted and tortured without anything close to the hard evidence that would be legally required to detain him in the US—was harrowing, but it wasn't unique. ██████████████
US military bases became dumping grounds for the CIA's cast-offs. Human beings were being bought, sold, and traded in the name of public safety and national security. They were taken from their families, wives, and children—often publicly kidnapped from streets or their homes. Operating in the shadows, the CIA used its influence and unlimited funding to capture and interrogate anyone it suspected. Soon the Agency was left with broken and beaten human beings with tales of brutal treatment. Risking exposure, the CIA pushed many of those prisoners into the military detainee system.
██████████████████████

Slahi's journey was typical. In July 2002 he landed in Bagram, the base that had sent personnel to Gitmo a few months previous to receive training in SERE tactics. New prisoners at Bagram arrived wearing hoods or blackout goggles and earmuffs, and were forcibly and immediately stripped of their clothes. While still hooded, with guards screaming at them, detainees would have their buttocks spread and cavities roughly searched. Many detainees shook as their interrogators screamed questions at them, not waiting for responses. Following additional interrogation in Bagram, Slahi was sent to Guantanamo a few weeks later. When he arrived at Gitmo on August 5, 2002, he weighed only 109 pounds and was given the internment serial number 760.

Slahi's arrival was also indicative of how Gitmo became a grotesque human scrap yard. Like ███████████, many of the detainees who ended up at Guantanamo had already been subjected to CIA and CIA-rendered interrogation before arriving. ████████ ██ ████████████████████████████. Basically, they would do anything to get the treatment to stop. Combined with the detainees US forces bought from Afghan warlords or tribes, Gitmo hardly was housing the worst of the worst. More like the leftovers. A detainee such as al-Qahtani, someone with real potential for intelligence gathering, was a rarity at Gitmo.

Slahi didn't rise to anything like al-Qahtani's level, but while hard evidence was slim to nonexistent in Slahi's case, there were deemed enough connections around him that he deserved a second look. From what we could gather, he was related to Abu Hafs al-Mauritani, who was a senior Al Qaeda figure and member of the group's inner Shura Council. In 1990, Slahi had also gone to college in Germany, during which time he had attended a mosque led by an imam associated with Egyptian Islamic jihad. This apparently radicalized him sufficiently that he joined the Mauritanian Muslim Brotherhood. Then, in 1991, Slahi had spent time at the radical al-Farouq training camp in Afghanistan, during which time he also swore an oath to Osama bin Laden. He joined jihad in Afghanistan against the Soviet-sponsored government as well as in Bosnia. He was also believed to have served as an Al Qaeda recruiter in Europe. There was also quite a bit of circumstantial information that placed him in the same areas as other suspects. What's more, we had some raw intelligence that suggested Slahi might have been involved in financial transactions with suspected Al Qaeda figures.

All that was enough for Slahi to be assigned to our CITF Planners and Financiers Unit to determine if there was enough actual evidence of nefarious activity to begin moving his case toward trial by the military tribunal, and we began to draw up an interrogation plan that employed our rapport-based techniques. Geoffrey Miller, though, had other ideas. By January 2003 he had picked up that Slahi had the potential to provide useful intel, and to get it out of him, his team developed an interrogation plan for Slahi that mirrored al-Qahtani's: dogs, water, forced grooming, denial of praying, blasting of music, environmental manipulation, and isolation.

Miller wasn't able to implement his plan immediately. Remember, the ruckus caused by Alberto Mora at the Pentagon had forced Jim Haynes and Donald Rumsfeld to temporarily withdraw approval for the EITs. That spring, however, after Rumsfeld had papered over Mora's objections with the report from his phony working group report, Miller got back in the game, and now he was ready to treat Slahi even more harshly. The new Behavior Management Plan proposed still crueler and more ridiculous treatment. By August 2003 Rumsfeld seemed confident that Mora's storm had blown over and approved Miller's new agenda.

Slahi was transferred into isolation and subjected to sensory deprivation. His few "comfort items," including legal papers and letters from his mother, were seized, and his cell was kept ice cold to add to his discomfort. Just as with al-Qahtani, JTF-GTMO's Battle Lab approach to Slahi was a failure. It produced no new information except what Slahi fabricated to ease his pain. Never willing to admit defeat, Miller's answer was to ramp things up and request approval for even harsher and more controversial techniques. The JTF-GTMO psychologists, interrogators, and other various self-appointed experts—people who had never even participated in intel exploitation until the previous year—had convinced each other they had developed a better way to extract the truth. If "breaking" a detainee didn't do the job the first time around, they would just break him a little harder at every subsequent round.

This time, the Defense Intelligence Agency, which by now had joined JTF-GTMO's interrogations, developed a plan for Slahi that centered on sexual assault, degradation, and religious humiliation. On July 1, 2003, Miller forwarded the new special interrogation plan up the chain of command, starting with SOUTHCOM. The general was going to show that he had more teeth than Slahi had ass.

Once again, Miller's abusive plans had supporters in high places. SOLIC's Marshall Billingslea, the same man who had told Mallow and Gelles they didn't know anything about interrogation, sent a handwritten note to Rumsfeld: "OGC concurs that this is legal. We don't see any policy issues with these interrogation techniques. Recommend you authorize." Rumsfeld did just that, putting his stamp of approval on the plan on August 1, exactly one year after the White House's August 2002 memo had very quietly legalized torture tactics.

The JTF-GTMO pseudo-BSCT intended to "condition" the detainee by making him respond to tasks. Slahi later gave testimony about his treatment. His account from his book *Guantanamo Diary*, which follows, was never officially confirmed, but it does conform to the methods and goals devised by the Gitmo pseudo-crew. At one point, he said, he was kept for days in a "secret place" in complete darkness and isolation:

I must not know the difference between day and night. I couldn't tell a thing about days going by or time passing; my time consisted of a crazy darkness all the time. My diet times were deliberately messed up. I was starved for long periods and then given food but not time to eat.

"You have three minutes: Eat!" a guard would yell at me, and then after about half a minute he would grab the plate. "You're done!" And then it was the opposite extreme: I was given too much food and a guard came into my cell and forced me to eat all of it. When I said "I need water" because the food got stuck in my throat, he punished me by making me drink two 25-ounce water bottles.

"I can't drink," I said when my abdomen felt as if it was going to explode. But [omitted] screamed and threatened me, pushing me against the wall and raising his hand to hit me. I figured drinking would be better, and I drank until I vomited.

All the guards were masked in Halloween-like masks, and so were the Medics, and the guards were briefed that I was a high-level, smart-beyond-belief terrorist.

"You know who you are?" said [omitted] friend. "You're a terrorist who helped kill 3,000 people!"

"Indeed I am!" I answered. I realized it was futile to discuss my case with a guard.

Slahi was also subject to sleep deprivation, but rather than being moved to a new cell every few hours, he was forced to drink a 25-ounce bottle of water every hour or two:

The consequences were devastating. I couldn't close my eyes for more than ten minutes because I was sitting most of the time in the bathroom. Later on, after the tension was relieved, I asked one of the guards, "Why the water diet? Why don't you just make me stay awake by standing up, like in [omitted]?"

"Psychologically it's devastating to make someone stay awake on his own, without ordering him," said [omitted]. "Believe me, you haven't seen anything. We have put detainees naked under the shower for days, eating, pissing, and shitting in the shower!"

Slahi reported that he was only occasionally hit, but JTF-GTMO clearly was trying as hard as they could to turn him into a broken human. Slahi was stripped naked and forced to stand. He was bent over so his anal cavity could be searched—yet another attempt to humiliate and sexually denigrate him. Other times, Slahi was beaten. Medical records documented rib contusions and cuts on his lip and head. He was placed in isolation, water was poured over his head, and he was subjected to temperature extremes, both cold and hot. Interrogators and guards bombarded him with strobe lights and blasting rock music to keep him awake. He was often kept in a room called the freezer. At other times, he was handcuffed to the floor with the air conditioner turned off and the hot tropical sun baking his cell.

The pseudo-BSCT also tried to use sexual taboos and violence to break Slahi. They told him his mother was going to be arrested and brought to Guantanamo, intimating that she would be brutally raped by the male prisoners. They had female interrogators pull off their shirts, rub their breasts on him, and grab his genitals. Devoutly religious, Slahi believed he was being raped.

One time Slahi was hooded and taken out into Guantanamo Bay in a boat for a mock execution. Interrogators told him, in Arabic, about how he was going to be killed and dumped overboard. That was enough to get him to piss his pants. Dunlavey's tenure had been notable for gross incompetence. Under Miller, that had been replaced by calculated sadism.

Later, resigned to spending his life in detention but hoping to stop the abuse, Slahi agreed to a confession:

"We know you came to Canada to bomb the U.S.," said [omitted].

"And what was my evil plan?"

"Maybe not exactly to harm the U.S., but to attack the CN Tower in Toronto?" he said. I was thinking, Is the guy crazy? I've never heard of such a tower.

"You realize if I admit to such a thing I have to involve other people? What if it turns out I was lying?" I said.

"So what? We know your friends are bad, so if they get arrested, even if you lie about [omitted] it doesn't matter, because they're bad." I thought, "What an asshole! He wants to lock up innocent people just because they're Muslim Arabs! That's nuts!" so [omitted] very much told me a precise crime I could admit that would comply with the Intel theory.

Slahi wasn't the only detainee being broken beyond all humane standards, for virtually no intel reward. On October 1, 2003, just days after Rumsfeld approved the plan for Slahi, Gitmo interrogators were also working hard to break another detainee, named Mohammed Jawad. He had become the focus of attention after being charged in Afghanistan with throwing a grenade at a military convoy, killing two Americans. After initially denying he was involved in the attack, Jawad "admitted" to the charge after Afghani authorities threatened to kill him and his family. He was sent to Gitmo, and when he arrived, he had a bone scan done that estimated his age at seventeen years old. (It is common in that part of the world not to keep strict track of age.) His family estimated he was much younger, and he sure looked it. Whatever his age—and the truth-fulness of his confession—Jawad could have been only an extremely low-level foot soldier, someone very unlikely to have any valuable information. Nonetheless, he had confessed to killing two Ameri-cans, so interrogating him became a higher priority than spending resources on the many other detainees who had ended up at Gitmo purely through bad luck or an Afghan warlord's spite.

After keeping Jawad for weeks in solitary confinement in dark-ness, one of the interrogators who had spent little time with Jawad before witnessed him having conversations with posters on the wall, not uncommon among detainees. When this same interroga-tor asked Slahi what it was like when he was held in dark isolation, he reported hearing voices that were "clear as crystal," including casual family conversation and someone reading the Koran in a heavenly voice. (Slahi also claimed the guards tried to exploit his state, talking to him through the plumbing and encouraging him to attack other guards.) Concerned about Jawad's mental state, the interrogator emailed Diane Zierhoffer, the psychologist provid-ing guidance on the boy's case. "It seems a little creepy," he wrote, wondering if the cause might be isolation from human contact and sunlight.

Zierhoffer wrote back that it was plausible. Sensory depriva-tion "can cause hallucinations, usually visual rather than auditory, but you never know," she wrote. Zierhoffer took no remedial action; instead, she advised him to double down on breaking Jawad. "He appears to be rather frightened," Zierhoffer wrote, "and looks as if he could break easily if he were isolated from his support network and made to rely solely on his interrogator. . . . Make him as un-comfortable as possible. Work him as hard as possible."

The team agreed to further isolate the boy, leaving him naked and sleep-deprived. Over a two-week period, Jawad was grabbed out of bed and moved to another cell every three hours. Miller would often tout this "frequent flyer" technique to visitors of the camp.

On December 22, 2003, Jawad—who had been moved out of isolation but was not allowed to have contact with the neighboring detainees—was accused of "cross block talk," a catch-all infraction that covered any attempt to make contact with anyone other than his keepers. His interrogators retaliated by taking the few remaining comfort items from Jawad's cell, including his prayer mat and Koran. For Jawad, like many detainees, prayer was the only solace he had. On Christmas Day 2003, Jawad attempted suicide by repeatedly banging his head against the metal walls of his cell.

By November 2003, more than three months after Rumsfeld had authorized new SERE-based interrogation plans—though now without the word "SERE" attached to them—the record of accomplishment was becoming starkly clear. For all their aggressiveness, the new plans produced little intel. But even so, Miller submitted requests to have the new programs used on additional detainees. General Hill had given his usual rubber stamp approval, and Assistant Secretary of Defense Billingslea consistently recommended Rumsfeld approve the plan. Detainee abuse at Gitmo was not the work of a few bad apples. It was expanding toward being the standard operating procedure for interrogation and being endorsed by policymakers at the highest levels. Torture was, in fact, becoming institutionalized.

Not that there wasn't pushback. At the CITF, we were aggressively questioning the ███████████████████████ ████████████████. Over at the Office of Legal Counsel, concerns were brewing too, about potential flaws in the August 2002 White House memo that had green-lighted so much of the horror show at Gitmo. This internal debate eventually came to a head when an OLC lawyer named Jack Goldsmith called top Pentagon lawyer Jim Haynes to advise him that the memo could no longer be relied upon as legal cover for enhanced interrogation.

Haynes and others had consistently relied upon that memo for their tenuous legal justification of what was going on at Gitmo, including overriding the concerns of top military lawyers such as Alberto Mora, but Goldsmith's objection presented a higher hurdle. Once Haynes relayed the OLC's opinion to Rumsfeld, the defense secretary could not legally sign off on Geoffrey Miller's newest request. The solution? An end run. Instead of sending Miller's request up to Rumsfeld for his signature, it was routed to his assistant, Deputy DOD General Counsel Daniel Dell'Orto, without telling him about the now-missing OLC legal cover. Dell'Orto signed off on the last day of 2003, and General Meyers approved the plan on January 2, 2004, assuring detainee abuse would continue in the New Year.

Far from being a new prison for a new kind of prisoner, Guantanamo Bay would become America's Devil's Island, or as Slahi would later describe it, Azkaban, the mythical fortress prison from the Harry Potter series. Within Gitmo's forty-five square miles, arbitrary imprisonment without legal recourse had become an instrument of national policy. All that was left now was to franchise the abuse throughout the war theater, and that was already in the works.

CHAPTER 11

ABU GHRAIB COUNTRY CLUB

The Iraq War that officially began with the "shock and awe" aerial assault of March 20, 2003, would grow quickly into a massive affair. More than half a million coalition forces, 309,000 of them American, led the invasion during the first year alone. Saddam Hussein was overthrown and eventually executed. His Baath Party had the government and military ripped from its hands. Baghdad's center city was transformed into a Green Zone—an American outpost in the midst of an occupied nation bristling with insurgents—while US and coalition forces spread far and wide across the country. A new government had to be formed, the people had to be pacified, a ruined economy and infrastructure needed to be brought back on line. Yet of all the people and places and stories that dominated the news in those days, one name stands out above all the others in memory: Abu Ghraib.

The Iraqi city of Abu Ghraib was a star-crossed place well before American interrogators turned it into a poster child for cruel and unusual punishment. Built in 1944 on the western edge of Baghdad—"Ghraib" may be a corruption of "gharb," Arabic for "west"—the city was best known for many years for its baby formula factory and for the suspicion, common among Western intelligence agencies, that the factory was also producing biological weapons. Severely damaged by Allied bombing during the first Gulf War in the early 1990s, the factory was partially rebuilt only to be bombed again and destroyed a decade later. On neither occasion, though, did the ruins contain any evidence of biological weapons or their manufacture. Indeed, the only compelling evidence ever discovered among the rubble were crates of baby formula.

The Abu Ghraib prison that US interrogators would make so famous was originally built by Saddam Hussein to warehouse his many political enemies. If its walls could talk, they would undoubtedly tell tales of prisoner abuse during those early years that would make even hardened torturers wince with pain, but that abuse was inflicted by a ruthless and sadistic dictator with no regard for international law, not by agents of a nation that had been one of the primary architects of the international conventions meant to prevent torturous acts.

Con men know that the secret of a great scam is to tell desperate people exactly what they want to hear, and by the late spring of 2003, more than a few people in high places in Washington were despairing about the situation in Iraq. The problem wasn't so much the war front, although the insurgency was gaining strength by the day, as it was the justification for the war already being fought. George Bush, Colin Powell, George Tenet, Dick Cheney, Donald Rumsfeld—they had all sold the invasion of Iraq to their own countrymen, to America's allies, and to the world at large via the United Nations as being necessitated, in part, by the presence of yet undiscovered WMDs and biological warfare weapons. The fact that none had been found—at the Abu Ghraib baby formula factory or anywhere else in Iraq—a full year into the war was beginning to suggest one of two things: either there were no such weapons and the evidence that there were, which had been obtained mostly by torturing detainees, was wrong; or indeed there were, and the only way to find them was to double down on and refine the torture already taking place at multiple military black sites across the country.

For pitching enhanced interrogation techniques, the timing couldn't have been better, or the conditions. Back in Washington, DC, Colonel Randy Moulton, the commanding officer of the Joint Personnel Recovery Agency (JPRA), was busy marketing SERE interrogation techniques and learned helplessness to the desk jockeys who were being pressed from above to find the thus-far-elusive evidence, both of WMDs and biological warfare weapons, and of an Al Qaeda–Iraq connection. The Defense Intelligence Agency and its purported interrogation experts were doing the same, within a command climate all too willing to ignore the fact that the JPRA, trained to recover military personnel, and SERE psychologists—experts in teaching American soldiers how to resist torture—had no real-world interrogation experience.

The Iraq Survey Group (ISG), which was formed in June 2003, at least spent time in the war theater, but ISG's charge was to find weapons of mass destruction, and that likely deafened members' ears to some extent to what they learned as they debriefed Iraqi prisoners, searching for evidence that would further their specific mission. Time and again those prisoners told the ISG they had been subjected to extensive cruel, inhumane, and degrading treatment by their military police officers and soldiers at multiple military camps in Iraq. At Gitmo, as we've seen, a thin legal fog hung over whether the Geneva Conventions against such practices actually applied. In Iraq, where the US was conducting an announced war, no such cover could be claimed. Nonetheless, the ISG failed to adequately flag what it must have witnessed—a program of intentional abuse intended to "set the conditions" for interrogation, exactly like the SERE EIT techniques at Guantanamo—and from there the practices involved began to metastasize through the entire war theater and, sadly, the insurgency as well.

ISG, though, had plenty of help, and it ran deep into the army command structure both in-country and out. At the time the ISG was established, army colonel Thomas Pappas was commanding the US Army's 205th Military Intelligence Brigade, which included the interrogators at Abu Ghraib. Initially those interrogators had been trained under the Army Field Manual at Fort Huachuca in Arizona. Unsatisfied with the results and seeking additional techniques beyond what his interrogators had learned under the AFM, Pappas assigned the task to Captain Carolyn Wood, his battalion assistant operations officer, as the officer in charge of the interrogation operations at Abu Ghraib. And this, in turn, completed the circle that connected Abu Ghraib and Iraq with Gitmo, black sites ███████████, and too much more. Wood, it turned out, had previously served as the interrogation operations officer at Bagram in Afghanistan, which had been the primary overseas testing ground for the unverified interrogation practices honed at Gitmo. It was also where Morgan Banks had been assigned, bringing with him his SERE methodology.

Will the circle be unbroken? I kept wondering, harkening back to the old spiritual and hoping it would. The answer, of course, was no. Not even close.

Captain Wood's assignment from Colonel Pappas had been to develop standard operating procedures for the military interrogators at Abu Ghraib. In July 2003 Wood simply adopted wholesale the

SOPs being used by the Special Mission Units already operating in Iraq, which were based on the SOPs being used by Special Mission Units in Afghanistan, which had been developed after their visit to—where else?—Gitmo. As Wood put it when she was questioned by the Senate Armed Services Committee, she had "cleaned up some of the grammar, changed the heading and signature block, and sent [the SOP] up" to be approved policy for the brigade. It didn't take long for the SOP to sink in. After the battalion Human Intelligence and Counterintelligence officer sought additional input on the SOP, he sent word around to this staff as follows: "The gloves are coming off gentlemen regarding these detainees. Colonel Bolz has made it clear that we want these individuals broken."

The response, thank goodness, was not universal approval. When Major Nathan Hoepner, the battalion's operations officer, received a draft of the orders, he looked at what the "gloves coming off" meant in practical terms: close-quarter confinement, sleep deprivation, white noise, and the use of dogs and snakes. Every officer in the command was allowed comments on the draft. Hoepner's were emphatic: "That in no way justifies letting go of our standards. We NEVER considered our enemies justified in doing such things to us. . . . BOTTOM LINE: We are American soldiers, heirs of a long tradition of staying on the high ground. We need to stay there."

In August 2003 Wood resubmitted her interrogation policy, including all the same techniques as her original proposal while omitting any negative responses such as Hoepner had provided. Wood even included an additional measure: sensory deprivation. That same month, following a phone call between JPRA Commanding Officer Moulton and the commander of the SMU Task Force in Iraq, a written request was sent to the JPRA for an "interrogation team." Now that the SMU had adopted the SERE EIT program as their interrogation standard, they needed training in how to apply it.

JPRA selected three people for the mission: Lieutenant Colonel Steven Kleinman; Terry Russell, the JPRA research and development manager; and Lenny Miller, a contract SERE instructor. The SMU specifically requested Lenny Miller be part of the support team. Of the three, only Kleinman was a trained and experienced interrogator, having previously served in that position in Operation Just Cause and Desert Storm. That alone was unique. In the army especially, but also generally across the services, interrogations are mostly done by junior enlisted personnel, many without college degrees. But Kleinman brought other skills to the party as well. As a former air force intelligence officer, he was well schooled in developing cooperative assets, and as the senior Joint Personnel Recovery Agency intelligence officer, he also was aware that his group was not designed or trained to handle interrogations. That, however, is precisely what Moulton had in mind for Kleinman's team.

Shortly after the team arrived in Iraq the first week of September 2003, Moulton authorized them to participate in SMU interrogations and to use the full range of SERE school physical pressures. Kleinman was taken aback by this. He thought he was being sent to Iraq to observe and offer advice on SMU interrogations, not to be in the middle of them. He was also concerned with the scope of the new rules of engagement. "How in the world did this get authorized?" Kleinman wondered.

On September 5, 2003, the JPRA team took part in its first SMU interrogation of an Iraqi detainee. When Kleinman walked in the room, he saw the detainee on his knees in a stress position and with a spotlight shining in his eyes, being repeatedly slapped in the face. A military police officer was standing in the background, menacingly pounding an iron bar on his hand.

Who is this guy? Kleinman asked himself. *He looks like a stereotype from an old gangster movie, slapping that bar in his hand.* When Kleinman was told this had been going on for thirty minutes, he felt it was a "direct violation of the Geneva Conventions" and "could constitute a war crime." Kleinman went to the SMU's immediate commander and recommended the session be halted immediately. He also called Randy Moulton and the SMU lawyer to remind them that the use of SERE tactics in an interrogation constituted violations of the Geneva Conventions.

Not so, Moulton replied. The JPRA team, he said, had been "cleared hot"—meaning there was full authority to proceed with SERE exploitation tactics in an interrogation.

Well, thought Kleinman, *Moulton is issuing an illegal order—service members have an obligation not to follow unlawful orders.* But in this opinion, he was on his own. His fellow team members, Russell and Miller, disregarded Kleinman's warnings and kept right on going, helping to abuse an Iraqi detainee with exploitation techniques from the SERE role-play scenarios.

To maximize the psychological impact on the victim, they told the detainee he was going to be released from custody. They let him clean up and walk out to a bus stop to wait for a ride home to his family. Thinking he was moments from freedom, the victim was roughly "captured" again by the SMU personnel. The two JPRA instructors then stripped him naked—other than the hood placed over his head and shackles on his wrists and ankles—and threw him into a cold, dark cement bunker. After that, they screamed at the victim and dehumanized him repeatedly. The guards were instructed to have the detainee remain standing for twelve hours, no matter how much he pleaded, unless he passed out.

Having witnessed the SERE exploitation tactics at work, Russell and Miller then proceeded, with Moulton's authorization, to develop a formal plan for using such practices on prisoners of war. Titled "Concept of Operations for HVT Exploitation," the plan was basically a DOD version of psychologist Bruce Jessen's April 2002 "Exploitation Draft Plan"—part of the EIT plan Jessen and Mitchell developed for the CIA.

Kleinman's warnings might have fallen on deaf ears, but his presence on the JPRA team remained a problem. Not only did he refuse to participate, he continued to let both the JPRA and SMU chains of command know they were engaging in what he considered criminal acts. Inevitably, this caused friction within and around the team—so much so that Kleinman remembers being threatened by an SMU member who, while sharpening his knife, warned Kleinman to "sleep lightly" because the SMU doesn't coddle terrorists. Not long afterward, a decision was made to extract the JPRA team from Iraq.

Steven Kleinman, it needs to be noted, was not alone in issuing warnings and vocalizing his opposition. At every step along the way to legitimatizing torture, brave, sometimes horrified people stepped forward—within the military, within the CIA, within adjunct civilian organizations such as my own, within government generally. Emails sent in June 2003 between CIA medical and psychological staff leave little doubt that concern over SERE-EIT practices ran high at Langley. Mitchell and Jessen, one email reads, "have shown blatant disregard for the ethics shared by almost all their colleagues."

The SMU task force legal advisor would later say he met with the SMU commander and told him SERE training was not meant for detainees. The lawyer also concluded that JPRA's presence had the potential to lead to abuse. He also said he told the commander JPRA was not qualified or trained to perform interrogations. The

SMU commander disregarded this legal advice, just as he did Kleinman's.

Further up the chain of command, Army Lieutenant General Robert Wagner, the Joint Forces Command J-1,* read in the September 4, 2003, *Weekly Report* about the new "gloves off" practices and about how some of his own JPRA people were involved in them and wrote back to the JPRA: "I'm not sure I see the connection between your assigned responsibilities and this task. It is a good observation and recommendation. But, what charter places JPRA in the business of intelligence collection?"

Similarly, when navy captain Daniel Donovan, the Joint Forces Command senior legal advisor, reviewed the JPRA plan for interrogating high-value targets, he responded back to Moulton that "even if Rumsfeld approved techniques for use in Guantanamo, where al-Qaeda and Taliban fighters were considered unlawful combatants, Iraqi prisoners fell under the full protection of the Geneva Conventions" and said interrogation techniques "would not be legal" in Iraq.

Donovan didn't give up there, though. On September 29, when he saw that general Wagner and chief of staff for joint forces command lieutenant general James Soligan might visit JPRA, Donovan alerted them that the Defense Intelligence Agency had approached JPRA about interrogation techniques and that the request "may have gone a bit further by asking JPRA to develop a plan for 'more effective' interrogations." Donovan notified the generals that the JPRA plan was "highly aggressive (such as the 'water board'), and it probably goes without saying that if JPRA is to include such techniques in a plan they prepare for an operational unit in another

---

* In military parlance, J-1 is responsible for Joint Forces manpower and staffing, J-2 for intelligence, J-3 for operations, J-4 for logistics, and J-6 for plans. The same system applies to the various branches of the service. N-1, for example, would be responsible for Navy manpower and staffing.

AOR, they need to be damn sure they're appropriate in both a legal and policy sense."

Ballsy patriots such as Nathan Hoepner, Steve Kleinman, Robert Wagner, and Daniel Donovan can be found in every war theater, in every age, but in Iraq and Afghanistan, at Gitmo, the Pentagon, and elsewhere, they were too few and far between as the summer of 2003 wore on. When Geoffrey Miller, the commander of advanced torture at Guantanamo Bay, showed up in Iraq in August 2003 "to discuss current theater ability to exploit internees rapidly for actionable intelligence," the deal was all but sealed. The fact that Miller had been hand-selected by the secretary of defense himself put the final imprimatur on the package: Gitmo was going global.

Miller had somehow convinced the Pentagon that his approach at Gitmo was successful and was the model others should be emulating. Even though it had no bearing in the Iraq War, where the Geneva Conventions applied, Miller brought with him the secretary of defense's April 16, 2003, policy guidelines for Guantanamo to serve as a model for the command-wide policy he recommended they establish.

When we at the CITF heard Miller was Donald Rumsfeld's choice for this key advisory role, we frankly couldn't believe it. The guy who presided over the aggressive expansion of torture at Gitmo was being sent to the front lines? What about the incredible controversy created when he began using the EITs at Guantanamo? More to the point, what about the total failure of that experiment in his Gitmo Battle Lab? For this, the Pentagon was going to expose him to a volatile operational theater?

But it no longer seemed to matter what interrogation professionals or lawyers said. When we alerted the Department of Defense's Office of General Counsel that Miller's trip would be an absolute disaster—that torture was a cancer and Miller was about to carry it into other theaters—we were told Rumsfeld personally selected Miller and there was no way to oppose the visit. Those in power, it seemed, were simply hell-bent on the notion that torturing prisoners was the way to do business. Somehow the Global War *on* Terror was becoming the Global War *of* Terror. We had turned into the very adversary we feared.

In case anyone had missed the point, Geoffrey Miller made it abundantly clear when he first met with the ISG's chief of interrogations at Baghdad International Airport's Camp Cropper. Miller asserted it looked like they were "running a country club."

"You're too lenient with the detainees," he added, then went on to recommend shackling the detainees; making them walk on the gravel rather than on the concrete pathways, to show them who was in control; manipulating room temperature; and one of his "innovations," depriving the detainees of sleep. After listening to Miller, one strategic debriefer assigned to the camp wrote a letter to his commander saying he would resign if they tried to implement the techniques Miller was recommending. Nonetheless Miller's advice—to "Gitmo-ize" the operation—began to echo throughout Iraq.

He had help: his legal counsel, Diane Beaver, also traveled with him to the Iraq Survey Group to spread the gospel. An SMU task force legal advisor told Beaver while she was in-country that he was concerned about the physical violence used during interrogations, including punching, choking, and beating detainees—later adding (shades of Steven Kleinman) that he was "risking his life" talking to her about these issues. But whether Beaver ever passed this news on to Geoffrey Miller is unknown. In 2007 Beaver would tell Senate investigators she had. For his part, Miller denied ever hearing about such concerns from Beaver.

What I do know for certain is that a slide presentation created following the ISG visit clearly showed that the group had discussed SMU "interrogation practices such as physical contact and choking." That same presentation further noted that other agencies, such as the CIA, wouldn't conduct interrogations in the SMU facilities due to prisoner treatment concerns. The detainee abuse, it turned out, was already rampant, widespread and accepted as a routine matter, even before Miller's arrival. That is perhaps understandable in a war theater. Violence begets violence. But Miller was dropping hints all over the place of what the official command position on detainee abuse would be going forward.

Major General Miller was going to push harsh, abusive interrogation even further—indeed, as far as he could. Forget Abu Ghraib Country Club. Captain Wood, who had been charged with creating standard operating procedures for the interrogators, understood that Miller and his team wanted to build a "miniature Guantanamo Bay" at Abu Ghraib prison.

Miller told Wood that the SMU plan for using the SERE EIT was a "good start" but that she should consider using something along the lines of what he had developed for Gitmo. According to one witness, Miller told Pappas, "These people are scared to death of dogs, and the dogs have a tremendous effect." (Miller later claimed he was not referring to using dogs in interrogations, just in the context of security operations. But if that was true, others took away a different message.)

Army Brigadier General Janis Karpinski, a military police officer from Rahway, New Jersey, oversaw the detention operations at Abu Ghraib. During Miller's August visit, he told her, "You're too nice. They don't know you are in charge. . . . You have to treat them like dogs," Karpinski also said Miller had told her: "We're going to change the nature of interrogation out of Abu Ghraib."

Before Miller left Iraq, he drafted new interrogation policies in a report titled "Assessment of DOD Counterterrorism Interrogation and Detention Operations in Iraq." In it, Miller wrote that if his recommendations were implemented, "a significant improvement of actionable intelligence [would] be realized within thirty days." Miller also recommended the detention guard force be subordinate to a new consolidated commander "that set the conditions for successful interrogations and exploitation of internees/detainees."

"It is essential that the guard force be actively engaged in setting the conditions for successful exploitation of internees," Miller wrote. "Joint strategic interrogation operations are hampered by the lack of active control of the internees within the detention environment."

Just as he had done at Guantanamo, Miller set about consolidating operations into one lean, unified torturing machine.

Last, Miller recommended establishing a BSCT to support interrogations because "psychologists and psychiatrists are essential in developing integrated interrogation strategies and assessing interrogation intelligence production."

Miller listed CITF's ███████████ as part of his visit team on his report, making it appear as if CITF somehow concurred with his findings. But although ███████ had been part of the team traveling with Miller, the general prohibited him from attending his meetings. "He's icing me out," ███████ told me in a phone call while he was still in-country.

Following his visit, Miller sent six personnel from Gitmo to Abu Ghraib to assist in implementing his recommendations and to establish a Joint Intelligence and Debriefing Center. On September 14, 2003, just a week after Miller left Iraq, Lieutenant General

Richard Sanchez issued a SERE EIT policy for the war region,
including Abu Ghraib. Just as Gitmo had called its EIT program
counterresistance strategies, Sanchez called his EIT program "interrogation and counter-resistance policy." The policy, he said,
"drew heavily" on what Rumsfeld had previously green-lighted for
Gitmo, including all of the twenty-four techniques Rumsfeld had
approved.

Initially, Sanchez authorized stress positions, sleep deprivation, load music and light control, and the use of dogs, as well as
techniques honed in Afghanistan after being originated at Gitmo,
effective immediately. That same day, still more interrogation techniques were appended. Anxious to begin, interrogators took turns
reading the guidelines line by line to each other. Not only had yelling, light control, loud music, deception, and false-flag operations
been green-lighted, but with approval from the interrogation officer or noncommissioned officer in charge, interrogators could now
also use stress positions, presence of dogs, dietary manipulation,
environmental manipulation, and sleep management.

By October 25 the interrogation repertoire for SMU Task
Force Iraq had been expanded still further to include the use of
controlled fear, environmental manipulation, isolation, and removal
of comfort items. None of these techniques were part of army interrogation doctrine or authorized by the Army Field Manual. Based
specifically on Miller's recommendation, military working dogs arrived at Abu Ghraib on November 20, 2003. According to a subsequent investigation, "abusing detainees with dogs started almost
immediately after the dogs arrived."

None of this had gone entirely unnoticed in the larger world. On
November 1, 2003, for example—six weeks after Sanchez approved
the EITs Miller had recommended and almost three weeks *before* the
dog abuse started—the Associated Press presented a special report

on massive human rights abuses at Abu Ghraib. But at the Department of Defense, such negative attention hardly seemed to matter.

To complete the "Gitmo-ization" of Abu Ghraib, in April 2004 Donald Rumsfeld personally picked Miller to be reassigned to Iraq as the deputy commanding general for detention operations. Now in command of both the military intelligence and military police functions in Iraq detention facilities, Miller essentially controlled the way detainees were to be treated in the entire theater. Just as Miller had hoped, his recommendations for abusive interrogation had been accepted wholesale, and he was in charge.

For Miller and the Department of Defense there was, however, one critical difference between Gitmo and Abu Ghraib. At Guantanamo, it was easy to control the spread of information within a US naval base operating on a heavily guarded little slice of an island in the Caribbean. On the other hand, Abu Ghraib was a prison just outside a huge city in the midst of a war zone filled with military and civilians coming and going, including people from many nationalities and international media.

In late 2003 and early 2004 British Special Forces soldiers returning from Iraq began reporting to the media that American private contractors were using SERE exploitation techniques in interrogations at Abu Ghraib, but "they didn't know what they were doing." Returning American service members began echoing some of their British counterparts, complaining about the abuses they were observing and ordered to participate in. Human rights groups were receiving hundreds of what they considered credible allegations of cruel, degrading, inhuman treatment. Some of those allegations were starting to arrive first-person, from detainees themselves. Their numbers kept growing; space at Gitmo and elsewhere was finite. Try as we might, we couldn't hold all of them forever, and once they were repatriated, many had stories to tell. By the time

Miller took command at Abu Ghraib, what had begun as a trickle of reports had grown into something the general would have a very hard time containing. Simultaneously, the accounts of repatriated detainees were helping fuel an insurgency that was beginning to surge out of control itself.

This wasn't because Miller was not afraid to push back. A few days after he took command, the *Guardian* reported that detainees were being subjected to "sexual jibes and degradation, along with stripping naked." Miller confidently "confirmed that a battery of 50-odd special 'coercive techniques' can be used against enemy detainees." The problem for Miller was that, while the cover from Department of Defense lawyers and psychologists made it seem the SERE interrogation tactics were technically legal, the techniques were still horrific. People outside of the military and intel bubble would know torture when they saw it. And that was only a matter of time.

As reports of Abu Ghraib abuse were leaking out, Afghanistan and Guantanamo Bay abuse stories also continued to be reported. Soldiers from the Afghani theater revealed the abuses were built into standard operating procedures. And the tactics, created by psychologists who theorized that learned helplessness would break a detainee's will to resist, actually did the opposite: they simply broke the detainee's will to live. Some elected suicide over subjugation. Others died or were killed (a semantic distinction in some cases) while in custody. Either way, they were useless as intel sources. Dead men don't talk.

The US Army Criminal Investigation Command (commonly known as CID) opened dozens of criminal investigations into detainee abuse as witnesses began to come forward and report on what they had witnessed, or had been part of. I had heard about some of the deaths, and rumors of more, and I had no doubt they were related to the Guantanamo Battle Lab and the SERE psychologists who had gone over to the dark side. After all, I had been reporting those same abuses for years. Still, I had no idea how rampant the abuse was at Abu Ghraib. Finally others were joining the cause, but the question remained: would anybody care this time?

CHAPTER 12

A PATTERN AND A SYSTEM

On January 13, 2004, US Army Specialist ███████, a twenty-four-year-old military police officer assigned to the Abu Ghraib prison, received an e-mail from an anonymous soldier. When ████ opened it, several photographs depicting horrific abuses at Abu Ghraib popped up on his screen—mistreatment of detainees at the hands of his own colleagues and friends.

████ was stunned, but driven by a sense of duty, he went to see ████████, who was a special agent with the CID assigned to Abu Ghraib. ████ gave the CID agent a CD of the photographs he had downloaded, irrefutable evidence of atrocities. The proof was documented, in fact, by some of the perpetrators. CID pledged to ████ that they would not disclose his identity. Then they opened a massive criminal investigation that would rock their own command, CENTCOM, the Pentagon, DOD, and well beyond.

Within a few weeks, CENTCOM informed the media that an official investigation had begun, involving the abuse and humiliation of Iraqi detainees by a group of US soldiers. On February 24, 2004, reports came out that seventeen soldiers had been suspended. The military announced on March 21, 2004, that the first charges had been filed against six soldiers. But in a media narrative still driven by terrorist attacks and the ongoing war in Iraq, none of these stories received significant coverage in the mainstream press.

The story was too explosive to be contained forever, though. Indeed, it only took a little more than a month—until April 28, 2004—for a *60 Minutes II* report filled with graphic images of abuse to blow the scandal wide open. Two days later, a Seymour Hersh *New Yorker* article detailing the abuses was posted online. After Hersh's reporting and the *60 Minutes II* photos, the unsettling abuse was injected into the mainstream consciousness. The images were so stark; there was no room to doubt that the United States was now a nation that tortured the people it captured.

For those of us who had been following the growth of harsh detainee treatment across the DOD, the disturbing actions of the military police captured in the photos had a name. They were clearly "setting the conditions" for the interrogations—just as General Miller had practiced in Gitmo and recommended during his trip to Iraq. The most famous photos released thus far depicted MPs Charles Graner, Lynndie England, Sabrina Harman, and Ivan Frederick posing over naked, dead bodies, some covered in their own feces and on dog leashes. Minus death, these were the same techniques Gitmo had developed for al-Qahtani and Slahi in 2002 and 2003. Other photos correlated to the psychological abuse developed at Gitmo as well: detainees handcuffed in stress positions, with underwear on their heads, or being threatened with dogs.

One of the most haunting images is of a hooded detainee standing on a box, his thin arms outstretched, wires taped to his fingers. He was held in this standing stress position by the threat that he would electrocute himself if he moved. This is exactly the type of psychological torture Albert Biderman described in his 1957 study of how communists had elicited false confessions from our prisoners of war. Back then, however, the North Korean POW camps were widely thought to be the worst, most inhumane places in the world. Now they had competition.

As more and more reports of widespread abuses came to light, the whole program started to unravel. Journalists began pelting the Pentagon with questions about detainee abuse. Rumsfeld and the Pentagon's public affairs staff were no longer able to control the narrative about the treatment of detainees. Their charm had worn off; the media began to recognize the level of manipulation and deception the DOD had relied on.

In damage-control mode, the Pentagon attempted to prevent additional disclosures. Rumsfeld tried to insulate himself by appointing his own investigations, trying to avoid any external look at the program designed under his authority. The secretary of defense's first such effort began shortly after ██████████ had reported the incriminating images he had received to army CID, but well before the dam had burst. On January 31, 2004, Major General Antonio Taguba was appointed to conduct a noncriminal investigation into detainee abuse in Iraq. However, Rumsfeld limited Taguba's scope to the 800th Military Police Brigade, the guards at Abu Ghraib.

Donald Ryder was appointed to assist Taguba. Well versed in Miller's complicity—as well as Miller's attempts to suppress any contrary position from the CITF—Ryder knew exactly where to look for evidence. Taguba's team reviewed photographs and videos and read fifty witness statements taken by Ryder's CID agents. The group also visited Iraq, inspected the Abu Ghraib prison, and spoke with additional witnesses. While Rumsfeld limited Taguba's scope, he couldn't easily stop him from carrying out his mission.

When Taguba filed his report in March 2004—still well before the floodgates opened—it contained multiple damning revelations about the "sadistic, blatant and wanton criminal abuses [that] were inflicted on several detainees" at Abu Ghraib between October and December of 2003. The report cited several MPs as well as members of two military intel battalions and the Joint Interrogation and Debriefing Center for having systematically abused detainees.

While some of the tactics Taguba reported conformed to the psychological abuses developed by the pseudo-BSCT at Gitmo, others seemed to be the horrific result of frustrated, bored, and angry guards who had been ordered to soften up the detainees. Some broke chemical lights and poured the phosphoric liquid on detainees' bodies; other prisoners were sodomized with lightbulbs. Male detainees were arranged in piles and jumped on; dead detainees on ice were photographed with smiling MPs posing next to them. Abu Ghraib also held some female inmates, at least one of whom was sodomized by a uniformed male guard.

Taguba also found that Abu Ghraib was holding "ghost detainees" for OGAs ████████████████████████ and moving them around in the facility to avoid detection by groups such as the International Committee of the Red Cross. "This maneuver was deceptive," stated the report, "contrary to Army Doctrine, and in violation of international law." Taguba was not authorized to investigate the military intelligence or CIA personnel involved, but he could document what he identified in the course of his investigation.

While the abuse at Abu Ghraib was already under way before Miller took over in March 2004, his impact on the nature of detainee treatment and interrogations was clear. Taguba's report included Miller's recommendation that "it is essential that the guard force be actively engaged in setting the conditions for successful exploitation of the internees."

Taguba also made specific the link between Miller's presence and rampant abuse. "I think it important to point out," stated the report, "that almost every witness testified that the serious criminal abuse of detainees at Abu Ghraib occurred in late October and in early November 2003." In other words, the sadistic and harsh treatment ramped up right after Miller visited Abu Ghraib and infected Iraq with the EIT and behavioral management process of detainee degradation. Taguba could not make any official finding about Miller, as he was beyond the scope of his investigation. But Miller's appearance in the report was probably as close to an indictment as Taguba could offer. Brigadier General Janis Karpinksi, head of military police at the prison, whom Miller had counseled to get tougher with the prisoners, was the only general officer at Abu Ghraib who was ever penalized. She was removed from her command and then demoted to colonel. Even then, neither action was officially related to the abuses at Abu Ghraib.

On March 24, 2004, within weeks of Taguba filing his report, Miller relinquished command of JTF-GTMO and left for Iraq. This was all as originally planned, but now with a different mission. Rumsfeld had initially picked Miller to Gitmo-ize the operations in Iraq. By the time the general arrived, however, his mission there had dramatically changed. Miller was now responsible for cleaning up the looming abuse scandal he had played a huge part in creating. Miller was appointed the deputy commander for detainee operations in Iraq, overseeing Abu Ghraib and other detention and interrogation facilities. It was the equivalent of Nixon sending H. R. Haldeman to investigate the Watergate break-in.

Not everyone was a villain in Taguba's report. ███████████, a navy dog handler, refused to participate in improper interrogations despite significant pressures from military intelligence personnel at Abu Ghraib. Private Joe Darby had, of course, turned over evidence to CID. First Lieutenant ███████████, an MP, took immediate action, stopped an abuse, and reported it. While the bravery of these three service members is commendable, the fact that Taguba was able to list only three individuals who stood up to the abuses is disturbing and reflective of the command climate there. It makes their moral fiber and courage even more noteworthy.

While Taguba's report was classified, it was leaked in late April 2004, causing further panic within the Pentagon. Rumsfeld wanted the allegations investigated, but he didn't want anybody to know the results.

Once the details in the report were widely publicized, congressional hearings were inevitable. Rumsfeld would have to try to cover his tracks. I don't know what Rumsfeld's lawyers told him directly. I was, however, present when his lawyers discussed that if Rumsfeld authorized the EITs at Guantanamo, he would be placing himself in jeopardy of possibly being tried internationally as a war criminal.

Of course, Rumsfeld wasn't the only one who might have been indicted for unlawful acts. Miller had followed through on Dunlavey's original request and had implemented the EIT program at Guantanamo. He had also infected Abu Ghraib and Iraq with the SERE EIT and detainee behavioral management program. The JPRA and SERE program were also on the verge of being exposed for their implementation of learned helplessness within the DOD. The Pentagon had been able to silence those of us at CITF, but the evidence of detainee abuse was mounting and the media would no longer be a pawn in the perception-management campaign. Rumsfeld, Miller, and the other DOD torture architects realized they were either going to sink or swim together.

As part of the expanding investigations, Morgan Banks was

ordered to come up to DC to explain his role in the now very public detainee abuse scandal. Afterward Banks called Larry James.

"General Miller wants you in Abu Ghraib," he told James. "He needs your help to fix the mess. Larry, I need to talk with you ASAP."

Miller got his way. Within two months of his arrival in Iraq, he brought James, his former JTF-GTMO BSCT chief psychologist, over. James had skin in the game too. He needed to insulate himself from the growing scandal.

With the leaking of the Taguba report, Rumsfeld was also forced to expand the scope of his reviews. He tapped Vice Admiral Albert Thomas Church, the naval inspector general, to investigate the detainee abuse scandal, this time including Gitmo. On May 4, 2004, I met with Church and laid out for him and his staff the DOD abuses that began with the establishment of JTF-170's BSCT and the Guantanamo Battle Lab. I told Church he needed to "find the logs"—the interrogation logs—not the sanitized reports JTF-GTMO was disseminating.

We had no idea how far people at the DOD or CIA were willing to go to cover up the abuse. But Britt Mallow felt we should have a backup printed copy of our important documents, in the event someone was able to purge our electronic records. I didn't tell Church about my backup plan: I had forwarded other copies of documents to trusted associates within NCIS for safekeeping.

On May 7, 2004, Donald Rumsfeld was called to testify before the Senate Armed Services Committee, which was holding hearings due to increasing media accounts of the mistreatment of Iraqi prisoners. "I feel terrible about what happened to these Iraqi detainees. They are human beings," testified Rumsfeld. "They were in US custody. Our country had an obligation to treat them right. We didn't, and that was wrong. So to those Iraqis who were mistreated by members of the US armed forces, I offer my deepest apology. It was inconsistent with the values of our nation. It was inconsistent with the teachings of the military, to the men and woman of the armed forces. And it was certainly fundamentally un-American."

Rumsfeld continued, "I wish we had known more sooner and been able to tell you more sooner, but we didn't." It was an audacious performance for someone who had hand-picked both Dunlavey and Miller to lead the Gitmo Battle Lab, sent Miller to Abu Ghraib, and worked to scuttle high-level legal reviews of the very torture tactics the committee was investigating. Rumsfeld knew he had blood on his hands, but there was no remorse in his conscience.

Two days later, on May 9, 2004, the Associated Press published a report with the headline PRISONERS' EARLY ACCOUNTS OF EXTENSIVE IRAQ ABUSE MET U.S. SILENCE. The article detailed allegations of psychological abuse, deprivation, beatings, and death at the US-run detention facilities under Miller. The AP also cited an army investigation documenting that "numerous incidents of sadistic, blatant and wanton criminal abuses were inflicted on several detainees." The Red Cross in Geneva made a rare public statement on the matter too: "We were dealing here with a broad pattern, not individual acts. There was a pattern and a system." An Iraqi provincial governor urged the US to stop the abuse, imploring, "What you are doing to the Iraqi people will turn against you!" And turn against us they did.

The next day in the *New Yorker*, Seymour Hersh reported on allegations of CIA domination at the prison as well as ghost detainees. The conspiracy was unraveling. If someone followed the trail, it would lead directly to the office of the secretary of defense, and maybe even the president. Alberto Mora had urged Jim Haynes to protect his client. Haynes didn't.

May 28, 2004, was my last official day as the CITF deputy commander and special agent in charge. By that time, it had become clear to me that the Bush administration had no real intention of bringing detainees to justice through a legitimate judicial process. I believe the administration had actually made that decision only three months after detainees began arriving at Gitmo. On April 5, 2002, British Prime Minister Tony Blair visited Bush at his Crawford ranch and pledged his unqualified support for an invasion of Iraq. From that point onward, Iraq became the administration's focus.

Over the next two years, the United States created a national policy of state-sponsored torture. I had spent too much of my time at CITF trying to stop the creation of these torture policies. I knew from hard-won experience that well-positioned people at the Pentagon and White House would go to any lengths to cover them up. I had even begun to feel like CITF was a decoy—a feint that we were going to bring terrorists to justice—more than a commitment to do so.

So I left the CITF having failed to bring Al Qaeda terrorists to justice or to ensure detainees were treated humanely. But I took every step I could to counter the illegal and inhumane activity at Gitmo. Despite my failures, I was able to leave with my integrity intact, knowing I fulfilled my oath to protect and defend the Constitution.

CHAPTER 13

"THE WORST OF THE WORST"

On March 10, 2005, US Navy Vice Admiral Albert Church testified before the Senate Armed Services Committee on the investigation he had led into allegations of detainee abuse at Guantanamo. Church told the committee: "Clearly there was no policy written or otherwise at any level that directed or condoned torture or abuse; there was no link between the authorized interrogation techniques and the abuses that in fact occurred."

I had a foretaste of this revisionism. Admiral Church had called me a few days earlier, after he briefed Defense Secretary Rumsfeld, to let me know the unclassified executive results of his findings were about to be made public and to thank me for my assistance. After all, my allegations had kicked off the process, and the logs I had shared with the Church committee had provided a factual basis for its investigation. But then Church moved on to an apology: "I can't believe that after you started it all, there was no interview of you recorded in the official report."

I was shocked. After Church and his staff had conducted more than 800 interviews of personnel in Afghanistan, Iraq, and Guantanamo Bay, my input didn't warrant inclusion? How could that be? Church explained this was an oversight, but then he made another curious statement. He said he was sure there would be additional investigations of the matter, most likely at the congressional level. In other words, he had just finished a voluminous report that unreservedly stated there was no policy of abuse, but he was certain the matter was far from settled. His strongest recommendation going forward, he assured me, was for future congressional investigators to interview me about detainee abuse. None of the subsequent Rumsfeld-appointed panels—and there were many of them—ever did.

I never found out if there was an actual order issued that no one was to talk with me. I just know I'd made allegations, a commission was formed, no one got back to me, and the issue I had raised—sanctioned torture—was basically whitewashed by a panel appointed by the man to whom my allegations might ultimately lead: the secretary of defense.

But that's pretty much how things went in the early days of pushback against what was happening at Gitmo, Abu Ghraib, and elsewhere. By the spring of 2004, the detainee abuses had widespread public attention. But after flurries of activity, everything would die down. Aside from a few soldiers, most of them far down the chain of command, no one had been held responsible. In fact, the people behind the EITs—not just the torturers themselves, but their facilitators back in Washington, in the DOD or at the Department of Justice, or at the CIA or elsewhere—still controlled the narrative: Torture was good. It was necessary, it was yielding actionable intel, it was protecting America from additional attacks. And, hey, if it sometimes got a little out of hand? Well, you have to break eggs to make an omelet.

What's more, these people also controlled the ultimate gateways through which internal protests had to pass. An example: In early 2005 Michael Chertoff was nominated by President Bush to replace Tom Ridge as the secretary of homeland security. Chertoff had been the deputy attorney general when many of the legal justifications for torture were being produced. He had also been one of the top lawyers who visited Gitmo and met with Dunlavey back in September 2002. Upon Chertoff's nomination, the American Civil Liberties Union called for an outside special counsel to investigate the exact role he had played in creating and implementing the Bush administration's torture policies. Unfortunately for the ACLU, their request landed on the desk of newly appointed US attorney general Alberto Gonzales. Not only had Gonzales been on the same Gitmo trip as Chertoff, as White House counsel he had also played a central role formulating and promoting the very interrogation practices the ACLU was protesting. The ACLU's request died on Gonzales's desk, the special counsel was never appointed, and Chertoff was unanimously approved by the US Senate on February 15, 2005.

Another example: . Apparently they did indeed ███████ because on November 9, 2005, Jose Rodriguez, the head of the CIA's Counterterrorism Center and RDI (Rendition, Detention and Interrogation) program, ordered that all the tapes be destroyed. His decision not only disappeared a smoking gun; it also defied an order from CIA director Porter Goss and resistance from senior US officials, including John Negroponte, then director of national intelligence. The destroyed videotapes were evidence of war crimes and violations of international and US law, but Rodriquez suffered hardly a whit for what he had done. What's more, Rodriguez was not held accountable by the Obama administration either. In 2010 the Obama Department of Justice decided not to press charges against Rodriguez for destroying the tapes.

Early on in this whole process, I had reminded my staff of what more than two decades in criminal investigations and counterintelligence work had taught me: there are no secrets, only delayed disclosures. My goal then had been proactive: do everything as if the whole world is watching, even when no one is in the room with you. At Gitmo—where so much took place beneath the radar, where observers from the International Committee of the Red Cross and even my own staff were not allowed to be—that turned out to be revolutionary advice. But it wasn't until 2006 that my advice appeared like it might also be correct.

That was the year the US Supreme Court ruled that the provisions of the Geneva Conventions did in fact apply to Guantanamo detainees. Specifically it called out Common Article 3 of the Conventions that includes the prohibition against cruel treatment, torture, and "outrages upon personal dignity, in particular humiliating and degrading treatment." Violations of Common Article 3 are deemed war crimes. Similarly, the War Crimes Act of 1996, enacted by the 104th US Congress, made "grave abuses" of detainees a violation of federal law. The Military Commissions Act of 2006 amended the 1996 statute by limiting "grave abuses" to torture, cruel or inhumane punishment, murder, mutilation, rape, sexual assault, or the taking of hostages.

Also in 2006 the United Nations Commission on Human Rights issued a report from a group of international experts, including the UN Special Rapporteur on Torture, Inhuman or Degrading

Treatment or Punishment. According to the report, the legal regime the US was applying to its detainees at GTMO "seriously undermine[d] the rule of law and a number of fundamental universally recognized human rights, which are the essence of democratic societies."

A nation's obligations under the Convention Against Torture allow for "no exceptional circumstances whatsoever, whether a state of war or threat of war, internal political instability or any public emergency may be invoked as a justification of torture." The UN report also recommended closing the Guantanamo detention facilities and called on the US to ensure all allegations of torture are investigated "and that all persons found to have perpetrated, ordered, tolerated or condoned such practices, up to the highest level of military and political command, are brought to justice."

UN reports have a way of dying slow, slow deaths, if they are even noticed, but the summer of 2008 was an election season, and a momentum was building that Washington couldn't ignore. In August of that year, the Department of Defense disbanded its Counterintelligence Field Activity, based on allegations of unauthorized collection of information on US persons and unlawful procurement practices. Although CIFA's budget and staffing were never made public, best estimates are that the agency spent more than $1 billion during its four-year existence and had perhaps 500 full-time employees and as many as 900 contractors working for it at the time it was closed.

Almost simultaneously, the Department of Justice's Office of Professional Responsibility issued a report titled "Investigation into the Office of Legal Counsel's Memoranda Concerning Issues Relating to the Central Intelligence Agency's Use of 'Enhanced Interrogation Techniques' on Suspected Terrorists." The report concluded that the FBI Guantanamo unit chief had indeed so advised that

Mohammed al-Qahtani be subjected to interrogation techniques, and that such advocacy "appears to conflict with the spirit if not the letter of Director [Robert] Mueller's instructions." It did much more than that. It helped contribute to the narrative created by the CIA that torture was necessary and effective. It may have also been a violation of the laws the FBI is responsible for investigating.

But the report was as notable for those who didn't sign off on it as those who did. David Addington, the former counsel to Vice President Cheney, and Timothy Flanigan, former deputy White House counsel under Alberto Gonzales, did not respond to requests for interviews. Attorneys for both CIA headquarters and the CIA Counterterrorism Center likewise declined to be interviewed in the investigation. So did Attorney General John Ashcroft.

Late December 2008 saw the release of the Senate Armed Services Committee report on detainee abuse, a document that explicitly spelled out the connections between detainee abuse in Guantanamo, Iraq, and Afghanistan and high-level authorization and cover-ups—exactly the dynamics I had spent two years of my life watching develop. The SASC report also laid out the story of how SERE techniques were repurposed for harsh interrogations.

In a letter accompanying the report's release, Michigan Senator Carl Levin, the chairman of the Senate armed services committee, recounted how he asked some questions of Jay Bybee, the former assistant attorney general for the Department of Justice's Office of Legal Counsel. On August 1, 2002, Bybee had issued two important opinions about the legal standards applicable to interrogations. One was sent to the White House, the other to the CIA. This much was already known; what was interesting was the backstory behind them. Not only did Bybee make clear that senior administration lawyers, including Alberto Gonzales, David Addington, and John Ashcroft, were consulted in the writing of the opinions, but so was the CIA itself.

In July 2002 the Agency had provided OLC with an assessment of the psychological impact of SERE-based interrogation techniques. Bybee wrote to Levin that the CIA assessment was used to "inform" his opinion about whether or not the techniques were legal. In essence, the top lawyers in the government were asking the CIA to tell them whether or not their program was abusive before they approved it. As Levin said, they "twisted the law to create the appearance of legality."

The SASC report also thoroughly debunked the claims of top administration lawyers and officials that the abuses were the result of a "few bad apples," concluding that, among other things, the well-known detainee abuses at Abu Ghraib in late 2003 "appeared in Iraq only after they had been approved for use in Afghanistan and at GTMO." The report also laid responsibility for the abuse at the feet of Donald Rumsfeld, whose "authorization of aggressive interrogation techniques for use at Guantanamo Bay was a direct cause of detainee abuse there . . . including military working dogs, forced nudity, and stress positions."

The granddaddy of all the reports on detainee abuse was the Senate Select Committee on Intelligence's "Report on Torture," one of the most comprehensive bipartisan congressional oversight investigations in history. The SSCI spent almost six years on the study and analyzed approximately 6.3 million pieces of documentary evidence from CIA cables, e-mails, briefing materials, memos, interview transcripts, and intelligence reports, as well as the CIA's own internal reviews of the program. When the 500-page executive summary of the report was made public on December 9, 2014, Dianne Feinstein stood on the floor of the US Senate and told her colleagues and the world the report "shows that the CIA's actions a decade ago are a stain on our values and on our history."

John McCain followed: The report, he said, is "a thorough and thoughtful study of the practices that I believe not only failed their purpose—to secure actionable intelligence to prevent further attacks on the US and our allies—but actually damaged our national security interests, as well as our reputation as a force for good in the world."

I couldn't agree more. Even in executive summary format, what became quickly known as the "Torture Report" is unequivocal in its findings and conclusions, which included:

1. The CIA's use of its enhanced interrogation techniques was not an effective means of acquiring intelligence or gaining cooperation from detainees.

2. The CIA's justification for the use of its enhanced interrogation techniques rested on inaccurate claims of their effectiveness.

3. The interrogations of CIA detainees were brutal and far worse than the CIA represented to policymakers and others.

4. The conditions of confinement for the CIA detainees were harsher than the CIA had represented to policymakers and others.

5. The CIA repeatedly provided inaccurate information to the Department of Justice, impeding a proper legal analysis of the CIA's Detention and Interrogation Program.

6. The CIA had actively avoided or impeded congressional oversight of the program.

7. The CIA impeded effective White House oversight and decision making.

8. The CIA's operation and management of the program

complicated, and in some cases impeded, the national security mission of other executive branch agencies.

9. The CIA coordinated the release of classified information to the media, including inaccurate information concerning the effectiveness of the CIA's enhanced interrogation techniques.

10. The two contract psychologists who devised the CIA's enhanced interrogation techniques also played a central role in the operation, assessments, and management of the CIA's Detention and Interrogation Program. By 2005 the CIA had overwhelmingly outsourced operations related to the program.

11. CIA detainees were subjected to coercive interrogation techniques that had not been approved by the Department of Justice or had not been authorized by CIA Headquarters.

12. The CIA did not conduct a comprehensive or accurate accounting of the number of individuals it detained and held individuals who did not meet the legal standard for detention. The CIA's claims about the number of detainees held and subjected to its enhanced interrogation techniques were inaccurate.

13. The CIA failed to adequately evaluate the effectiveness of its enhanced interrogation techniques.

14. The CIA rarely reprimanded or held personnel accountable for serious and significant violations, inappropriate activities, and systemic and individual management failures.

15. The CIA marginalized and ignored numerous internal critiques, criticisms, and objections concerning the operation and management of the CIA's Detention and Interrogation Program.

16. The CIA's Detention and Interrogation Program was inherently unsuitable and had effectively ended by 2006 due to unauthorized press disclosures, reduced cooperation from other nations, and legal oversight concerns.

17. The CIA's Detention and Interrogation Program damaged the United States' standing in the world, and resulted in other significant monetary and nonmonetary costs.

In August 2014, while the CIA was publicly criticizing the conclusions in the "Torture Report," the Agency quietly conceded many of the issues raised there in a "public" document called "Note to Readers." In the note, the CIA admitted it had misrepresented the importance of information obtained from Khalid Sheikh Mohammed (KSM) and that in some cases, it already possessed the information purported to be "unavailable" prior to KSM's interrogation. The CIA also admitted it misrepresented the number of detainees in custody and did not notify the secretary of state of all of its black-site prisons, and it further acknowledged that information used by President Bush in a 2006 speech was in error.

Such admissions are rare in the Agency's history, and this one was clearly meant to be hard to see. Even the Senate Intelligence Committee was unaware of the note's existence for at least a year after it was first made public. Except for the alert attention of

BuzzFeed journalist Ali Watkins, the CIA's correction for the record might well have gone completely unnoticed.

The takeaway from all these reports and investigative panels: The progress forward—away from condoning torture and protecting torturers—has been painfully slow and incomplete. Tens of thousands of pages of articles, reports, programs, and documents covering the matter have been printed in the past decade or so, some of them with fascinating, even horrifying revelations. But the record on holding those responsible for the abuses accountable for their actions has been spotty at best. What follows is a sampling.

ARMY MAJOR GENERAL MICHAEL DUNLAVEY
First commanding officer of the Joint Task Force 170 at Guantanamo

Dunlavey started the abusive Behavioral Science Consultation Team and applied to expand enhanced interrogation techniques, such as locking up detainees, restricting human contact including doctors, shackling detainees to the floor, and leaving them shivering in the cold. A lawyer and state judge, Dunlavey added his legal opinion to the EIT request, stating: "I have concluded that these techniques do not violate US or international law."

After being relieved of his command at Guantanamo in November 2002, Dunlavey became the assistant director for homeland security at the CIA. During his time there, he contacted Britt Mallow to see if he could visit the CITF headquarters on Fort Belvoir. Mallow said no—he was persona non grata.

Dunlavey retired from the army in 2004 and returned to his position as a judge of the Pennsylvania Court of Common Pleas for the 6th Judicial District, based in Erie, Pennsylvania. In 2012 he retired. In November 2016 Dunlavey spoke to a veterans group in support of Donald Trump's selection of retired army lieutenant general Michael Flynn as national security advisor.

LIEUTENANT COLONEL DIANE BEAVER
Counsel for Joint Task Force 170 at Gitmo

Beaver's flawed legal arguments were used as cover for torture at Guantanamo. After leaving Gitmo, she was promoted to the staff of the Pentagon's Office of General Counsel.

Beaver was later called to testify before the Senate Armed Services Committee (SASC), where she faced tough questioning from Missouri senator Claire McCaskill about her suggestion that interrogators be granted "advance immunity."

"What planet are we on?" asked McCaskill. "There is no such thing as 'immunity in advance.' That would be a crime."

Beaver also said she believed there were no violations of law at Gitmo, adding that detainees "were beaten to death at Bagram, Afghanistan."

McCaskill replied: "It's a sad day in this hearing room when we say, 'Well, it's not that bad. At least they weren't beaten to death.'"

Under questioning by other senators, Beaver claimed she wasn't a military justice expert and that she had been hung out by the SOUTHCOM staff judge advocate. She further claimed she was "shocked" that her opinion "would become the final word on interrogation policies and practices within the Department of Defense."

When asked about Beaver's legal opinion during the same hearings, Alberto Mora testified, "I knew instantaneously, sir, that this was a flawed policy decision based upon inadequate legal analysis." When asked if other staff judge advocates shared Mora's views, he replied: "Sir, every judge advocate I've ever spoken to on this issue shared that view."

A *Toronto Globe and Mail* review of the documentary movie *The Guantanamo Trap: Four Ways of Looking at Torture* wrote that Beaver "looks like any suburban neighbor, in a polo shirt and Bermuda shorts" before going on to note she will go down in history as "the torture lady."

Beaver was last known to be practicing commercial litigation for the Bryan Cave law firm in St. Louis, Missouri.

MAJOR ███

Psychologist on the Behavioral Science Consultation Team at Gitmo

Although he had no training in interrogation when he arrived at Guantanamo, ███ helped give medical cover for the SERE-base enhanced interrogation tactics that were used there. ███ cowrote a paper detailing three categories, culminating with tactics such as twenty-hour-a-day interrogations and acting out mock executions. ███, who has a PhD in psychology, then became personally involved in the dehumanization of Mohammed al-Qahtani, including giving advice on how to break down the detainee and assessing al-Qahtani to ensure his abuse could continue.

In 2013 a psychologist and ethical campaigner named Trudy Bond asked the American Psychological Association to investigate ███ role in torture at Guantanamo. The Center for Justice & Accountability also asked the APA to expel ███. The APA has declined both requests.

Complaints were also filed against ███ license to practice psychology in the state of New York. The NY attorney general concluded ███ "apparently, was asked to use his skills as a weapon;

not to help the mental health of the detainees." However, since there was no "therapist-patient" relationship between ████ and the detainees, he did not consider ████ behavior the "practice of psychology" under New York law.

MAJOR PAUL BURNEY
Psychiatrist on the Behavioral Science Consultation Team at Gitmo

Like ████, Burney helped give medical cover for the SERE-based enhanced interrogation tactics at Guantanamo. In addition to working with ████ on a paper detailing three categories of interrogation tactics for approval, Burney became personally involved in al-Qahtani's abuse. He was present when al-Qahtani was stripped, when he was forcibly groomed, when a female interrogator invaded his personal space, when he was threatened with a military working dog, and when he was treated like an animal.

When interviewed by the Senate Armed Services Committee in 2008, Burney admitted the purpose of his and ████ 2002 trip to Fort Bragg was to find out how to use brutal SERE tactics for interrogations at Guantanamo. Burney said Morgan Banks was fully aware that the purpose of the visit was to "see if we could use SERE tactics to try to elicit information from detainees."

Burney is currently a psychiatrist in Menasha, Wisconsin.

LIEUTENANT COLONEL DIANE ZIERHOFFER
Psychologist on the Behavioral Science Consultation Team at Gitmo

Zierhoffer consulted on the case of teenage detainee Mohammed Jawad. She noted that Jawad ████████████████████████

██

██████████████████████████████████████ Zierhoffer
then recommended to the interrogators: ███████████████
███████████████████████████

When called to testify in Jawad's military commission hearing, Zierhoffer invoked her right against self-incrimination and refused to testify about her role in encouraging the detainee's regimen of sleep deprivation, prolonged isolation, or other involvement in aiding, abetting, and encouraging detainee abuse.

During the trial, Jawad's defense counsel, USAF Major David Frakt, said, "What has this country come to when a licensed psychologist, a senior officer in the US armed forces, someone trained in the art of healing broken hearts and mending broken minds, someone with a duty to do no harm, turns her years of training and education to the art of breaking people, to the international devastation of a lonely, homesick teenage boy?"

Frakt also stated that Zierhoffer's written report was "one of the most chilling documents that has been produced so far."

Zierhoffer is currently a psychologist at the Department of Defense.

DAVID BECKER
Chief of the Interrogation Control Element at Guantanamo
for the Defense Intelligence Agency

Becker served as a surrogate for General Dunlavey in enthusiastically advocating for the use of EITs at Gitmo, repeatedly citing their effectiveness in Afghanistan. Becker specifically requested SERE training for the military interrogators. Among other interrogation tactics the DIA officers used was forcing detainees to watch gay pornography and wrapping them in the Israeli flag.

Becker is currently a senior executive at the Department of Defense.

ARMY LIEUTENANT COLONEL JERRY PHIFER
General Dunlavey's intelligence chief

Phifer worked with Becker to promote the use of EITs at Guantanamo, purporting they were essential for mission accomplishment. Jerry Phifer personally approved the SERE training, with the specific intention of using those tactics on al-Qahtani. Just as the CIA had done, Phifer argued that the detainees possessed critical intelligence that could save lives and that the detainees had sophisticated counterresistance training and were thus able to defeat traditional interrogation practices. No useful intelligence was ever extracted at Guantanamo using these tactics.

Phifer currently works for intelligence contractor InCadence on a project for the DIA.

██████████

CIA ████ counsel

████████ counseled General Dunlavey's torture architects on the legality of aggressive interrogation in October 2002, helping torture spread from the CIA black sites to Guantanamo. Among the advice ████████ offered about torture laws was, "the language of the statute is written vaguely. . . . Severe physical pain [is] described as anything causing permanent damage to major organs or body parts. Mental torture [is] described as anything leading to permanent, profound damage to the senses or personality. It is subject to perception. If the detainee dies, you're doing it wrong."

At the Senate Armed Services Committee hearing, Michigan senator Carl Levin expressed his own shock at ████████ "advice." "'If the detainee dies, you're doing it wrong'? How on Earth did we get to the point where a senior US government lawyer would say that whether or not an interrogation technique is torture is 'subject to perception' and that if 'the detainee dies, you're doing it wrong'?"

████████ is currently a member of the Council on Foreign Relations and a senior lawyer in the CIA Office of General Counsel.

MAJOR GENERAL GEOFFREY MILLER
First commander of the unified Joint Task Force Guantanamo

Miller applied for and oversaw the increasingly aggressive torture techniques under his command. In late October 2003 Miller visited Abu Ghraib. During his visit, he insisted the treatment of detainees wasn't harsh enough and that the prison should be "Gitmo-ized" so detainees could be broken psychologically. In April 2004 Secretary of Defense Rumsfeld picked Miller to become deputy commanding officer for detention operations at Abu Ghraib.

In 2006, when two soldiers were facing charges for using dogs to intimidate prisoners at Abu Ghraib, Miller was called to testify. Miller asserted his Fifth Amendment right not to incriminate himself. Later that year, Miller retired from the US Army as a major general. At a ceremony in the Pentagon's Hall of Heroes, the army vice chief of staff presented him with the Distinguished Service Medal for "exceptionally commendable service." Miller was also praised as an innovator.

In 2013 Miller was banned from entering the Russian Federation for alleged human rights violations.

In 2014 two former Guantanamo Bay prisoners asked a French judge to investigate "war crimes and acts of torture inflicted on detainees" at Guantanamo, including issuing a subpoena for Miller. In 2015 the Paris court of appeals approved a request for Miller to appear for questioning. Miller did not respond.

In 2016 French magistrates again issued a subpoena for Miller to answer questions about his role in the detention and torture of former Guantanamo detainees Mourad Benchellali and Nizar Sassi. Miller did not reply to the summons or appear in court.

Miller is currently retired.

DAVE BRANT
Former director of NCIS

Brant played an important role in supporting CITF's attempts to block torture from becoming policy at Guantanamo. He retired from NCIS in 2005 after leading the agency through the attack on the USS *Cole* and the 9/11 attacks. Brant is currently CEO at the National Law Enforcement Officers Memorial Fund and Executive Director at the National Law Enforcement Museum.

MIKE GELLES
NCIS operational psychologist

Gelles trained interrogators in rapport-based approaches and was actively involved in the early pushback against the abusive tactics embraced by other psychologists. Gelles is the author of the book *Insider Threat: Prevention, Detection, Mitigation, and Deterrence.* He is currently managing director at Deloitte consulting. For his service to the CITF, Gelles was awarded the US Army Civilian Public Service Award and Medal.

BOB MCFADDEN
NCIS special agent

Arabic speaking and extremely knowledgeable about Al Qaeda hi-erarchy, Bob trained our team in the Middle Eastern mindset and rapport-based interrogations. Like Mike Gelles, he was awarded the US Army Civilian Public Service Award and Medal for his service to CITF. Bob is currently a senior manager at Deloitte consulting.

RALPH BLINCOE
NCIS deputy director

Blincoe resisted Dunlavey's attempts to advance torture as policy. In 2010 Blincoe began his second career, as a law enforcement and counterintelligence consultant for both corporate and government clients. He led a yearlong study into the use of the polygraph in the Department of Defense. Blincoe is currently the senior consultant to the Department of Defense Insider Threat Management and Analysis Center (DITMAC), and in this capacity he works closely with Mike Gelles and Bob McFadden, who are also consultants to the project.

COLONEL STEVE KLEINMAN
Air force intelligence officer and former CIA agent

Kleinman reported and refused to participate in abusive inter-rogation in Iraq. He has testified before congressional hearings and continues to work closely with behavioral scientists on interrogation-related research.

Kleinman was a founding member and is the current chair of the High-Value Detainee Interrogation Group (HIG) research committee, succeeding me in that position. He also serves on the executive committee for the International Investigative Interviewing Research Group. Kleinman is an active spokesman against torture on behalf of Human Rights First and was named by that organization to the list of Nine Heroes Who Stood Up Against Torture.

Kleinman retired from the US Air Force in March 2015.

SERGEANT JOSEPH DARBY
Whistle-blower who gave a CD with images of abuse at Abu Ghraib to army CID

Darby was promised anonymity by army CID, but his cover was publicly blown when Defense Secretary Rumsfeld mentioned him by name on national television. Darby faced a mixed reaction from the other members of his unit. After receiving death threats, he was evacuated from Iraq under armed guard and held in protective custody. His wife also faced persecution at home, including threats to her husband and graffiti on her property. After being released from protective custody, Darby and his wife relocated to an undisclosed town.

In 2004, Darby was selected as one of three ABC News People of the Year. He also received a John F. Kennedy Profile in Courage Award in 2005.

ARMY COLONEL LOUIS "MORGAN" BANKS
SERE psychologist at Fort Bragg who provided training for ███████, Paul Burney, and others from Guantanamo Bay in 2002

The training Banks provided became instrumental in developing the three categories of interrogation tactics used on detainees at Gitmo. General Miller wrote that Banks later came to Guantanamo to conduct an "assessment visit" on the Battle Lab and that he had provided "very valuable insights." Banks also spent four months in 2001–2002 at Bagram, the airbase in Afghanistan where detainees were—often brutally—processed for shipment to Guantanamo.

As of this writing, Morgan Banks still holds the contract to instruct Behavioral Science Consultation Team psychologists at the Army Intelligence Center in Fort Huachuca, Arizona.

COLONEL LARRY JAMES
Army psychologist

James became personally involved in the spread of, and medical justification for, torture at both Guantanamo and Abu Ghraib. James recommended his former protégé, ███████, for General Dunlavey's Behavioral Science Consultation Team. He later arranged for ██ to meet Morgan Banks, who set up the SERE-based interrogation training sessions. In 2003 James became the chief psychologist for Guantanamo's interrogation team. In 2004 he became director of the behavioral science unit at Abu Ghraib before moving back to Guantanamo in 2007.

In 2008, James published *Fixing Hell*, in which he describes an interrogation he watched from behind a one-way mirror at Abu Ghraib: "The prisoner had been forced into pink woman's panties, lipstick and a wig; the men then pinned the prisoner to the floor in an effort to outfit him with the matching pink nightgown." In response James "poured a cup of coffee, and watched the episode play out, hoping it would take a better turn and not wanting to interfere without good reason."

James is currently the dean of the School of Professional Psychology at Wright State University in Dayton, Ohio, as well as a Council of Representatives member of the American Psychological Association, division of military psychology. Along with Morgan Banks, James remains a strong advocate for the Behavioral Science Consultation Team's role in interrogations.

MOHAMMED AL-QAHTANI
Alleged twentieth 9/11 hijacker and inmate at Guantanamo

Al-Qahtani was the first test case for SERE-based interrogation techniques at Gitmo. He was interrogated and tortured for fifty days in the Guantanamo Battle Lab between November 2002 and January 2003. He was further held in an isolation cell until April 2003. In an attempt to gain control over him, interrogators subjected al-Qahtani to sexual abuse, beatings, temperature extremes, and humiliations based on religious and cultural beliefs.

Attempts to bring charges against al-Qahtani have failed. In early 2008 charges were entered only to be dropped that May. Al-Qahtani was recharged in November 2008. Two months later, on January 14, 2009, Judge Susan Crawford, the convening authority for military commissions, publicly acknowledged al-Qahtani would not be referred to trial due to his torture. "We tortured Qahtani," Crawford said. "His treatment met the legal definition of torture. And that's why I did not refer the case." It was the first time the Bush administration had admitted to torture; the admission came one week before a new president was sworn in.

Soon after taking office, President Obama ordered the closure of Guantanamo Bay. Al-Qahtani was one of seventy-one individuals who fell into a strange legal limbo. Although it was unlikely the government could win a trial against him, he was still considered too dangerous to release. Obama set up a periodic reviews board, representing various US national security agencies, to review the information available on this category of detainee. Al-Qahtani was denied approval for transfer on July 18, 2016. He has been held at Guantanamo for more than fifteen years.

MOHAMEDOU OULD SLAHI
Mauritanian, suspected Al Qaeda member, inmate at Guantanamo

Slahi became the second Guantanamo prisoner slated for the same kind of abusive interrogation program as al-Qahtani. Under General Miller's command, Slahi was beaten, sexually abused, and subjected to a mock execution, repeated water dousing, and temperature extremes.

Slahi learned English in prison, and in 2015, *Guantanamo Diary*, a handwritten diary of his treatment at the hands of his American captors, was released. The book became an international bestseller, although Slahi was not allowed to have a copy.

In July 2016 a periodic review board concluded that Slahi had never posed a "continuing significant threat to the security of the United States." His almost fourteen years in detention were based more on a fear that he would reveal his treatment at Guantanamo. On October 17, 2016, Slahi was released and returned to Mauritania.

MOHAMMED JAWAD
Teenage detainee at Guantanamo

Following an abusive interrogation by Afghani authorities, Jawad confessed to throwing a grenade at US troops and was transferred to Gitmo. After showing signs of depression and hallucinations, Jawad was targeted for extreme treatment by psychologist Diane Zierhoffer, including complete isolation and being moved from his cell an average of every three hours for two weeks. Jawad attempted suicide on Christmas Day 2003.

During Jawad's military commission proceedings in August 2008, his defense counsel, USAF Major David Frakt, argued that the US started "down a slippery slope, a path that quickly descended, stopping briefly in the dark, Machiavellian world of 'the ends justify the means,' before plummeting further into the bleak underworld of barbarism and cruelty, of 'anything goes,' of torture."

On July 30, 2009, the US district court for the District of Columbia ordered Jawad's release. The next day, the Office of Military Commissions dismissed the charges against him. On August 24, 2009, after six years, Jawad was released from custody at Guantanamo and returned to Afghanistan.

A few months after his release, Jawad was interviewed by the English-language United Arab Emirates–based newspaper the *National*. Asked about the war in his native Kabul that had heightened while he was away, Jawad answered, "The situation will get worse because it's impossible to finish fighting with fighting. It's impossible to clean blood with blood."

GUL RAHMAN
Afghan detainee

On March 28, 2010, the Associated Press identified Rahman as the CIA prisoner who had frozen to death eight years earlier while being held at a secret ████████ detention facility ████████ ████. Rahman had been rounded up with ████████████

██

██,
Rahman is said to have been violently uncooperative, at one point even throwing a latrine bucket at his captors. For that, his hands were shackled over his head.

████████████████████████, Rahman was in his unheated cell, stripped naked from the waist down, when the temperature dropped to near freezing. Within hours, he was dead. A CIA on-site medic determined the cause of death was hypothermia.

██

██

██

██ In
Rahman's case, the CIA inspector general investigated the death and said those in charge of the interrogation had used "poor judgment" in leaving the prisoner exposed to harsh weather. When the case rose to the attention of Kyle Foggo, then the Agency's third-ranking officer, he refused to take any action against Rahman's captors. Two federal prosecutors who also looked into his death concluded that no CIA officer involved in the incident had meant to intentionally harm Rahman. Rahman's body was never returned to his family for burial. No one at the CIA has ever been held responsible.

JOHN WALKER LINDH
US citizen captured in November 2001 during the
US invasion of Afghanistan

Lindh, known in the media as the American Taliban, was held at Camp Rhino before being transported to the USS *Peleliu* in December 2001. His secret shipboard detention was challenged by the ACLU.

On February 5, 2002, Lindh was indicted by a grand jury for ten charges, including conspiracy to murder American citizens and supporting terrorist organizations. He pleaded not guilty to all charges. Proceeding with the case would have allowed Lindh to testify in public about any abuse he had suffered during interrogation. On July 15, 2002, Lindh accepted a plea bargain carrying a twenty-year term. He could be released as early as 2019.

JAMES MITCHELL
JOHN "BRUCE" JESSEN
SERE psychologists turned CIA contractors who were the co-fathers of enhanced interrogation techniques

Mitchell and Jessen's paper "Recognizing and Developing Countermeasures to Al-Qa'ida Resistance to Interrogation Techniques: A Resistance Training Perspective" introduced the concept of using abusive SERE techniques to overcome reputed Al Qaeda interrogation resistance training. These included an attention grasp, shoving a detainee into a wall, and grabbing and slapping a detainee. The psychologists recommended a detainee be placed in a cramped and dark confinement box and that insects could be placed inside the boxes to exploit any potential phobias. Mitchell and Jessen's work was the cornerstone of the tactics used by CIA interrogators at black sites.

Some of the CIA officers observing the use of these EITs during the interrogation of Al Qaeda suspect Abu Zubaydah were disturbed by them. CIA correspondence describes them as being "profoundly affected . . . some to the point of tears and choking up." Two of three of the CIA personnel there wanted to be transferred from the facility if the torture of Zubaydah continued. Those involved reported Zubaydah "was unable to effectively communicate" and that he "cried," "begged," and "whimpered" due to his torment.

When asked to evaluate their program's effectiveness, Mitchell Jessen & Associates reported that the manner in which Zubaydah was tortured served "as a template for future interrogations of high-value captives."

In November 2016 Mitchell's book *Enhanced Interrogation: Inside the Minds and Motives of the Islamic Terrorists Trying to Destroy America* was released.

There have been numerous calls for investigation and prosecution of Mitchell and Jessen, including a 2014 editorial in the *New York Times* and a 2015 request by Human Rights Watch. In 2015 the American Civil Liberties Union filed a lawsuit against Mitchell and Jessen.

Mitchell is retired and lives in a wealthy suburb of Tampa, Florida.

Bruce Jessen is retired and lives in a $1.5 million house outside Spokane, Washington.

AMERICAN PSYCHOLOGICAL ASSOCIATION
Largest professional organization for psychologists in the United States

The APA has repeatedly refused calls for its members involved in abusive interrogations to be held accountable. The APA's role in promoting torture as an interrogation tactic was revealed in the fall of 2014 by *New York Times* reporter James Risen's book *Pay Any Price: Greed, Power and Endless War*. Risen focused on the billions being spent by the military and intelligence agencies on APA-member contractors, as well as James Mitchell and Bruce Jessen's role in justifying torture.

The APA responded that Risen "touches on an ugly period in

our nation's history, one in which longstanding principles of human rights were violated," adding that "his conclusions about the APA are largely based on innuendo and one-sided reporting." In response to continued criticism over psychologists' involvement in torture, the APA commissioned an independent review called the Hoffman Report.

The Hoffman report found that APA leadership actively colluded with government torture programs, often by simply ignoring what was happening. The report states, "APA intentionally decided not to make inquiries into or express concern regarding abuses that were occurring, thus effectively hiding its head in the sand."

For example, when one APA member tried to file an ethics complaint against James Mitchell in 2005, "the complainant contacted the Ethics Office several times prior to filing her complaint against Mitchell and that each time an Ethics Office staff member discouraged her from filing the complaint." When she persisted and her complaint was finally accepted, an Ethics Office staff member found there were three James Mitchells who were APA members and no further steps were taken. Mitchell resigned from the APA nine months later while the complaint was still pending. In recent years, the APA also declined to take action against ███████.

The publicity generated by the *New York Times* coverage of the Hoffman Report finally broke down the APA's resistance. On July 14, 2015, the board of directors announced the retirement of the APA chief executive officer and deputy CEO, as well as their executive director for communications. Other officials were removed or fired, and others retired or resigned.

The APA membership demanded further action. At its August 7, 2015, annual conference in Toronto, the Council of Representatives voted overwhelmingly to prohibit psychologists from participating in national security interrogations. The vote was 157–1. The one vote against was from Larry James, the psychologist who had served at Guantanamo and Abu Ghraib.

None of the psychologists involved in the development of enhanced interrogation techniques have had their membership revoked or received other disciplinary action.

ALBERTO MORA
General counsel of the navy

Mora led a three-year campaign at the highest levels of the Department of Defense, attempting to prevent the acceptance of any legal justification for abusive interrogation tactics. Mora could not stop all torture, although he prevented al-Qahtani and other Guantanamo inmates from being waterboarded.

Mora left the government in 2006, the same year he was awarded the John F. Kennedy Profile in Courage Award. He has served as international counsel to Walmart and vice president, general counsel, and secretary to Mars, Inc.

Mora is currently a fellow at the Carr Center for Human Rights at Harvard University's Kennedy School. One of his projects there has been an extensive analysis of the cost and consequence of torture. The study disclosed that US and Iraqi officials had concluded that more than 90 percent of the suicide bombings in Iraq between 2003 and 2005 were from foreign fighters. It was clear that the treatment of detainees at Guantanamo Bay and Abu Ghraib helped attract foreign fighters to the battle. These suicide attacks killed thousands of people, both Americans and Iraqis. When American contractor Nick Berg was beheaded by Abu Musab al-Zarqawi in 2004, Al Qaeda in Iraq claimed it was in retaliation for Abu Ghraib.

DONALD RUMSFELD
Secretary of defense

Rumsfeld was an enthusiastic and active proponent of the development of torture as a policy within the Department of Defense. Rumsfeld hand-picked both General Dunlavey and Miller to run the Guantanamo Battle Lab. He later chose General Miller to travel to Abu Ghraib to encourage illegal and abusive interrogation and detention policies. Rumsfeld then selected Miller to take over detention and interrogation at Abu Ghraib, just as the media began to break stories about illegal abuse and torture in the prison. Rumsfeld resigned as secretary of defense in 2006, amid criticism for his military planning.

Rumsfeld has been the subject of repeated lawsuits in the United States based on prisoner abuse during his time as secretary of defense. In 2007 a federal judge dismissed a suit brought by the ACLU, claiming Rumsfeld could not be "held personally responsible for actions taken in connection with his government job."

In December 2014 the European Center for Constitutional and Human Rights filed criminal complaints in Germany accusing Donald Rumsfeld of war crimes. The complaint included the case of Khalid El-Masri, a German citizen who was captured by CIA agents in 2004 due to mistaken identity and tortured at a secret prison in Afghanistan.

Rumsfeld is currently retired and lives in New Mexico.

WILLIAM "JIM" HAYNES
General counsel to the Department of Defense

Haynes worked closely with Rumsfeld as a principal legal architect of the use of torture in interrogation, including at Guantanamo. Haynes resigned from the DOD in March 2008 to become chief corporate counsel to Chevron. On October 12, 2016, the European Center for Constitutional and Human Rights and the New York–based Center for Constitutional Rights urged a French judge to subpoena Haynes based on a complaint of torture, abuse, and arbitrary detention of two former Guantanamo detainees.

Haynes is currently general counsel and executive vice president at SIGA Technologies, Inc.

KYLE "DUSTY" FOGGO
Executive director, CIA

On September 29, 2008, "Dusty" Foggo pleaded guilty to felony corruption charges in federal court. ████████████████████ ██ ██████████████████████████████████████, in which the CIA tortured detainees. Court papers disclosed a record of misconduct on Foggo's part stretching over twenty years. He has never been held accountable for those actions.

GEORGE TENET
Director, CIA

CIA director during the adoption and spread of EITs as well as a vocal proponent of the war in Iraq, Tenet announced his retirement as director on June 3, 2004, just as the controversy over the flawed intelligence leading up to the war with Iraq was heating up. That December, President Bush presented Tenet with America's highest civilian award, the Presidential Medal of Freedom. Tenet today is managing director of Allen & Company, an investment bank.

SENATE SELECT COMMITTEE ON INTELLIGENCE REPORT
Also known as the "Torture Report"

The full report of the Senate Select Committee on Intelligence, to-taling more than 6,500 pages, is still highly classified and has never been made public. It was, however, sent to the White House, CIA, DOJ, DOD, State Department, and to the office of the director of national intelligence, and its conclusion is now in the public record: "This and future Administrations should use this Study to guide future programs, correct past mistakes, increase oversight of CIA representations to policymakers, and ensure coercive interrogation practices are not used by our government again." Nonetheless, senior executives in many of the agencies to which the report was sent, including the FBI, ordered their personnel not to open or read it.

When Republican senator Richard Burr replaced Democrat Dianne Feinstein as chairman of the SSCI after the 2014 elections, he went further, demanding agencies return all copies of the full SSCI report to the Senate, claiming they never had a right to see the report in the first place.

Amid concern all copies of the full report will be destroyed, President Obama announced he will have a copy of the report preserved in his presidential library, guaranteeing the survival of at least one copy. However, the report will remain classified until at least 2028.

ISLAMIC STATE OF IRAQ AND THE LEVANT (ISIS, ISIL, OR DAESH)
Terrorist organization

Beyond extreme and regressive religious orthodoxy, Daesh has also claimed to be motivated by the US invasion of Iraq and torture of

Muslims. The precursor group to Daesh rose to prominence during the Iraqi insurgency following the US invasion of Iraq. Countless reports since have chronicled the barbaric treatment of prisoners in Daesh custody, including dressing them in orange jumpsuits—replicating Guantanamo detainees—and waterboarding only the US and UK hostages to emphasize the US treatment of Islamic prisoners. Abu Bakr al-Baghdadi, the Daesh cult's emir, met many of Daesh's future leaders in detention at the US prison Camp Bucca in southern Iraq. The *New York Times* describes the prisons as "virtual terrorist universities: The hardened radicals were the professors, the other detainees were the students." Thousands of former detainees around the world share at some level a deep sympathy with what al-Baghdadi reportedly told his captors as he was leaving Camp Bucca: "I'll see you in New York."

GTMO
American naval base that became infamous globally for prisoner abuse and torture

As early as May 2006, George W. Bush started talking about the need to close Gitmo. "I very much would like to end Guantanamo; I very much would like to get people to court," he told reporters. One of Barack Obama's first acts as president was to pledge to close Gitmo. On January 22, 2009, his second day in office, Obama issued Executive Order (EO) 13492, directing that the detention facility be shuttered "as soon as practicable, and no less than 1 year from the date of this order."

The president returned to the subject in his January 20, 2015, State of the Union Address: "We have a profound commitment to justice—so it makes no sense to spend three million dollars per prisoner to keep open a prison that the world condemns and terrorists use to recruit. Since I've been president, we've worked responsibly to cut the population of GTMO in half. Now it's time to finish the job. And I will not relent in my determination to shut it down. It's not who we are."

Colin Powell has said closing Gitmo is "in the best interest of the nation." Retired generals, admirals, and national security professionals have publicly advocated for closure, yet the prison remains open as I write, home to 41 remaining detainees, being held now at a per-person cost of nearly $11 million annually. Worse, the war criminals who fostered and practiced torture there have yet to be held accountable for their actions.*

Miami Herald journalist Carol Rosenberg, who has covered Gitmo since the arrival of the first detainees, has dubbed those who remain "forever prisoners." As one who was there at the beginning,

---

* The interim report of the United Nations Special Rapporteur on torture and other cruel, inhuman or degrading treatment or punishment, for which I served as a consultant, properly extends accountability to those who witnessed detainee torture and remained mute on the subject. Specifically, the report states:

> "The obligation to report mistreatment should be enshrined in national law, with appropriate sanctions for non-reporting and protections for those who report. The duty to report should be extended to violations of other standards and safeguards, including the prohibition against compelling detainees to confess, incriminate themselves or testify against others, and subjecting them to coercion, threats or practices impairing their judgment or decision-making capacities.

> "All violations, including of the right to be properly informed of one's rights and to legal assistance, must be impartially investigated upon complaint and subject to appropriate sanctions. The protocol should consider prospective remedies and sanctions, such as disciplinary or administrative action and obligation to undertake additional training, for breaches of standards and attendant procedural safeguards designed to prevent the use of coercive interviewing practices."

I'm in full accord. It does seem like it was forever ago when Gitmo first opened, and some days it seems like Gitmo might go on forever more. But I also believe we have to think about "forever prisoners" in a broader sense, to include ourselves, our national values, and the undeclared war that shows no sign of ending.

War crimes were committed at Gitmo—that's indisputable. According to the SSCI Torture Report, the "evidence is overwhelming and incontrovertible," yet the conspiracy of silence continues, just as it continued for so long in the Nixon administration after the Watergate break-in burst into the headlines. Cover-ups, compliant White House counsels, stonewalling, using the CIA to achieve political objectives, unlawful acts, the use of special units, and the need for a special prosecutor to get the truth out—it all sounds so very familiar, and maybe it should. Two of the principal architects of our torture policy post-9/11 learned their craft during Watergate at Richard Nixon's knees: Dick Cheney, who first came to the White House in 1970 as a staffer to the director of the office of economic development during Nixon's first term and would go on to become George W. Bush's vice president; and the director Cheney first worked under in the White House, Donald Rumsfeld, defense secretary to Cheney's VP when EITs were first born.

Maybe given that history, it was inevitable the CIA's fabricated claims of torture success at their black sites would combine with flawed legal analysis, ambitious commanders, and convenient psychologists to turn Gitmo into a symbol of torture, injustice, and oppression that still haunts not just America but all of the West. But I was there at the creation, and like a lot of others, I couldn't stop it all from happening. That thought will haunt me for a long time to come.

CHAPTER 14

A DISASTER FORETOLD

I wrote earlier that the series of legal decisions that would ulti-mately be used to justify torture unfolded like an avalanche wit-nessed in slow motion. You could clearly see it coming, you could wave your arms and yell, but ultimately there wasn't a damn thing you could do to stop it.

I wouldn't see the series of contracts that James Mitchell and Bruce Jessen had signed with the CIA for almost a decade and a half after they came into existence, but when I finally did, I realized how easily, almost casually, all this had begun.

Here, for example, are snippets from an August 21, 2002, mod-ification to an existing CIA contract with Mitchell that had been set to expire on August 31. The modification extended the contract to the end of the year:

"Sponsor [CIA] has a need to identify reliable and valid methods for conducting cross-cultural psychological

assessments. . . . Sponsor has a need to identify current
state of the art behavioral sciences research and methods of
influencing attitudes, beliefs, and behavior across cultures."

The "objective" of the project under contract would be
to "identify and describe the reliability and validity of existing methods and strategies for conducting cross-cultural
(including non-English speaking, non-Western cultures)
psychological assessments under dynamic conditions, with
limited access to the individual being assessed, short turn
around [sic] time for completion of the assessment and
high degrees of ambiguity and uncertainty stemming from
conflicting or incomplete data, biased presentation and
multiple information sources."

To that end, Mitchell was to:

- "Identify the current state of behavioral science on theories
  and methods for influencing attitudes, beliefs, motivation and
  behavior;

- "Describe the reliability and validity of existing techniques,
  methods and strategies for motivating and influencing human
  behavior, particularly those which can be used for motivating
  and influencing individuals from non-Western cultures;

- And "Identify and describe the reliability and validity of existing methods and strategies for determining which method of
  influence is most likely to be effective for a given individual."

It's all so bland, so technical, so filled with the language of
contracts and the catch words and phrases of psychology. But
the reality of this bloodless document, of these "cross-cultural . . .

psychological assessments under dynamic conditions," was the sweaty cells in which exhausted, haunted, brown-skinned men lived like animals, some for more than a decade. The reality was interrogators throwing Mohammed al-Qahtani a mock birthday party and then forcing him to watch a puppet show depicting him having sex with Osama bin Laden. The reality was dirt farmers from Afghanistan rounded up wholesale and shipped to the American Azkaban in the sparkling Caribbean.

Ultimately, Mitchell and later Jessen's contracts would be renewed and added to because people, some guilty and some innocent, were being systematically destroyed in hidden spots around the world, and because too many other people who watched all this with personal distaste, even horror, saluted and marched on.

By late October 2002, I had been exposed to one too many similar documents—legal opinions, meeting summations, written orders filled with antiseptic, almost Orwellian language for what I knew in my heart and through observation to be horrible and inhumane practices. After reading one of them—the minutes of a meeting I describe in chapter 7—I sent the following e-mail to ████████████, our senior legal advisor and the senior command staff at the Criminal Investigation Task Force. It reads in part:

A lot of us did, in fact, consider how history would judge these actions. My memo was far from the only one raising a yellow flag. Alberto Mora was heroic in his opposition to the torturers. This book has introduced you to plenty of others who put their careers on the line or sought out journalists after they were back from combat to say loud and clear: "What we have seen is wrong!"

Clearly, though, those voices were not enough. The boulder kept rolling. The avalanche followed. America became just what its extremist enemies wanted—a fellow terrorist in a world where the established rules of war no longer applied.

We know the truth of what happened now, and the facts of the extraordinary efforts that were made to keep that truth hidden from the American public forever. We know because people such as Senators Dianne Feinstein and John McCain wouldn't turn their eyes away from what was happening or be cowed by the powerful protectors of the torture secrets.

As early as 2005, McCain used his stature as a former Vietnam War POW to lead a bipartisan effort that resulted in the successful enactment of the Detainee Treatment Act—also known as the McCain Amendment—that prohibits torture and other cruel, inhumane, and degrading treatment of those held in US custody.

Nine years later, in 2014, Feinstein, who was then head of the Senate Select Committee on Intelligence, refused to back down when it became apparent the CIA was "spying" on her committee's investigation of Agency torture practices. Instead, she gave a March 2014 speech on the Senate floor expressing her concerns that a CIA search of the Senate computers "may well have violated the separation of powers principles imbedded in the United States Constitution."

Feinstein also refused to back down a month later, in April 2014, when former CIA director Michael Hayden said in an interview on *Fox News Sunday* that she was being too "emotional" about the torture subject. Watch torture sometime; it's an emotional spectacle.

Others didn't back down either, and I fought along with them. In a November 16, 2010, letter to then-Defense secretary Robert Gates, I joined Steve Kleinman, ███████████, ex-CIA field officer Robert Baer, former FBI counterintelligence agent Joe Navarro, and nine others in condemning the "Appendix M" that was added in 2006 to the Army Field Manual on interrogation tactics and practices. Among other ill-considered changes, Appendix M authorizes interrogators to place detainees in pitch-black goggles and earmuffs for periods of up to twelve hours, which can then be extended with permission of a flag or general officer, and to prevent detainees from sleeping more than four hours a day for up to 30 days in a row.

"As interrogators, interviewers and intelligence officers with decades of experience in the field, we believe that these interrogation tactics are ineffective," we wrote. "Furthermore we recognize that they can be counterproductive (i.e., they can serve to enhance rather than reduce both the detainee's resistance while also severely diminishing his ability to accurately recall critical intelligence information). The use of these techniques was clearly banned in previous versions of the manual and they ought to continue to be clearly off limits."

Have we won that fight yet? No, but that's no reason to quit. In fact, it's every reason to keep going.

In the same spirit, in an April 2012 op-ed for the *Huffington Post* titled "Torture Is Illegal, Immoral, Ineffective and Inconsistent with American Values," I took on Jose Rodriguez, who had argued in his book *Hard Measures* that torture was necessary and saved lives. I challenged Rodriguez's claims and argued that the misguided tactics had actually hardened resistance, an outcome that another half decade of brutal war has proven deadly accurate.

I also challenged the media as a whole to stop referring to enhanced interrogation techniques as "what human rights advocates call torture," as if this were some kind of battle between tree huggers and national security experts. Narrative matters, and media plays a huge role in shaping how the public perceives events. One of the key jobs of journalism is to look behind the curtain of intentionally bland phrases such as "enhanced interrogation techniques." Once *60 Minutes II* and Seymour Hersh pulled that curtain back— once they showed the world that EITs and torture were too often synonymous—there was no going back to ignorance. But that could have and should have happened sooner.

In October 2014 Human Rights First convened a panel of seventeen of the nation's most respected interrogation and intelligence professionals, including former US military general officers and senior executive service members. I was involved in getting the word out and personally called and e-mailed many of them to ask that they participate. After much deliberation, we sent out to the media a statement of principles that torture is illegal, ineffective, and counterproductive. We followed that up with interviews and an open letter to President Obama that I helped draft, urging him to instruct the current leadership of the CIA to unequivocally stand behind his condemnation of torture. Eventually, we consolidated all those materials onto a website, humanrightsfirst.org, that the media and public generally could access.*

Two months later, on December 8, 2014, I wrote an op-ed for *Politico* titled "Dick Cheney Was Lying About Torture." The op-ed was a further challenge to the narrative Cheney and other torture apologists kept peddling in their incessant effort to convince the public of the necessity and effectiveness of the CIA Rendition, Detention, and Interrogation program. My purpose, I said, was to illuminate the darkness about torture. Beyond that, the larger purpose of all this activity was to redirect the narrative about torture, and I think we managed that. And my timing couldn't have been better: about twelve hours after the *Politico* column was released, the "Torture Report" was introduced on the Senate floor, and the narrative about EITs was forever changed.

President Obama acknowledged as much at a televised White House press conference on October 1, 2014, when he stated, "We tortured some folks. . . . We did some things that were contrary to our values."

The president went further in his January 20, 2015, State of the Union address when he said, "As Americans, we respect human dignity, even when we're threatened, which is why I've prohibited torture."

In one of his last official documents—a January 19, 2017, letter to Speaker of the House Paul Ryan and President Pro Tempore of the Senate Joe Biden—the president expanded his critique to the broader harm Gitmo has inflicted on America's security and standing in the world: "Rather than keep us safer, the detention facility at Guantanamo undermines American national security. Terrorists use it for propaganda, its operations drain our military resources

---

* http://www.humanrightsfirst.org/topics/interrogators

during a time of budget cuts, and it harms our partnerships with allies and countries whose cooperation we need against today's evolving terrorist threat." Gitmo, he wrote, is "a facility that never should have been opened in the first place."

In retrospect, given how Gitmo evolved, I couldn't agree more with that last point, but President Obama also hedged his bet on more than one occasion when he discussed the CIA and torture. We "crossed a line," he allowed, but added that it was important "not to feel too sanctimonious" because those responsible for torturing detainees were working during a period of extraordinary stress and fear.

With that last sentiment, I have to take serious exception. Yes, these were times of extraordinary stress and fear, but as the old saying goes, character is what you do when no one else is looking, and what the CIA and its aiders and abettors did when no one else was looking was flat-out wrong.

Faith counts—faith in core values and founding principles, in our constitutional framework, and the rule of law. The torturers had no faith in the faith that matters.

Leadership matters too, but rank, title, and grade level are no guarantee of talent or meaningful experience. Following bad orders given by incompetent (or worse) bosses is not leadership; challenging the order is. If only the torturers had done more of that.

Loyalty is important too, but loyalty to core values, not to individuals. When core values are being violated, as they were time and again in the treatment of detainees at Gitmo and elsewhere, challenge is the purest form of loyalty.

And finally strategy: it must be supported by tactics, not dragged down by them, and it must be aimed at realistic outcomes consistent with values.

On every one of those fronts—faith, leadership, loyalty, and strategy—our detention and interrogation policies, promulgated and endorsed at the highest levels of American government, came up woefully short, in ways that harm us still. What makes this even worse, and more painful for me, is that we had the proper way to do this right in front of us, and we had proof positive that rapport building with detainees yields infinitely more usable intelligence than beating the shit out of them—or fucking with their minds. But tough guys were in charge, the ones with more teeth than ass, and too many of the tough guys hunkered behind their desks in Washington couldn't get enough of them or their dismal, unproven "science"—with sadly predictable results.

Torture ended up making us less safe as a country, not more so. Indeed, the most significant threat to our national security post-9/11 has come not from second waves of attacks from Al Qaeda or fresh waves of terror from ISIS but from the very manner in which the CIA and other agencies administered their interrogation program and from the ready willingness of Donald Rumsfeld, Dick Cheney, the Defense Intelligence Agency, the DOD's Office of General Counsel, and others to turn their backs on international conventions regarding the treatment of detainees. The cancer that began at Guantanamo Bay and later metastasized to Abu Ghraib didn't stop there, or in Afghanistan either. Evidence mounts every day that the CIA's black sites were a near-global phenomenon that compromised officials all around the world, or forced them to look away from horrendous acts.

███████████████████████████████████████
███████████████████████████████████████
███████████████████████████████████████
███████████████████████████████████████
██████████████████████████
███████████████████████████████████████
███████████████████████████████████████
███████████████████████████████████████
███████████████████████████████████████
████████████
███████████████████████████████████████
███████████████████████████████████████
███████████████████████████████████████
███████████████████████████████████████
██
███████████████████████████████████████
███████████████████████████████████████
███████████████████████████████████████
███████████████████████████████████████
███████████████████████████████████████
██████████████

In January 2015 the former chief of staff to Secretary of State Colin Powell publicly disclosed that the US had used ███████ ███████████████, as one of the CIA black sites where detainees were tortured. Now, there are renewed calls in ████████ to investigate ████████ involvement in the torture of detainees.

Yes, "we tortured some folks," as President Obama said so colloquially back in 2014, but it wasn't just "we." The "American way of torture" dragged way too many people all around the world down into the pit with us, and it continues to do so to this day.

Gitmo remains open—the Forever Prison for Forever Prisoners—

and seemingly it now has a fresh advocate in the White House. At a Nevada campaign stop in February 2016, Donald Trump vowed to keep Guantanamo Bay open and fill it "with some very bad dudes." Far more alarming to me, Trump has also spoken approvingly of reinstituting waterboarding and even using "much tougher" techniques on all these very bad dudes he apparently intends to detain at Gitmo. To quote Trump from another 2016 campaign stop: "Torture works. OK, folks? Believe me, it works. . . . And waterboarding is your minor form, but we should go much stronger than waterboarding."

No, President Trump, it does not work. In fact, it has just the opposite effect. Waterboarding, sleep deprivation, dog leashes, sexual humiliation—they all send us tumbling into the filth where our sworn enemies live, and it legitimizes their struggle in the eyes of their followers even as it delegitimizes us in the eyes of the world. The challenge now is to regain the high ground, not double down on the low road. This book is my effort to illuminate the mistakes we made and to help elevate us above them so we can return to the values that have so long made the United States of America the envy of the world. America has always been strongest when our actions match our values.

ACKNOWLEDGMENTS

I want to thank the entire Regan Arts team for its support, most especially Kathy Huck and Judith Regan, who believed that a book about how we enacted state-sponsored torture needed to be written. Many publishers felt torture was a dead issue until the election of Donald Trump as president brought the issue back onto the front pages.

This book would not be possible without the support of Sterling Lord Literistic and my agent, Robert Guinsler, who from the very beginning believed this story needed to be told. I'm grateful for the fantastic editing of Nathan and Howard Means, who helped polish my manuscript and turn it into a book, as well as Patrick McCord for his advice and contributions. Pamela Hamilton has been so much more than a publicist. She has been by my side throughout the writing and editing process and has acted as coach, mentor, and friend. I'm also grateful to my brother, Bill Fallon, for his tireless efforts and assistance with web pages, branding, and other materials to enable my message to reach a broader audience.

I am so grateful for the encouragement, mentoring, and friendship of Bill Dedman, Jess Bravin, Josh Phillips, and Adam Grant.

Their guidance and assistance with book proposals and finding an agent, publisher, and editors helped make this book possible. They continue to be a frequent source of council and guidance.

I'm also humbled to count heroes like Dave Brant, Ralph Blincoe, Steve Corbett, Mike Gelles, and Bob McFadden among my closest friends, and I'm profoundly grateful for the incredible amount of time they took helping ensure the accuracy of the details in the book. Britt Mallow, Scott Johnson, Sam McCahon, and other CITF terrorist hunters helped me piece together the amazing role we played in our history.

Roy Nedrow, John McEleny, Neill Robins, Pete Segerstein, Steve Schiebinger, Ron Struble, Blaine Thomas, Stu Couch, Carol Joyce, Randy Carter, Steve Minger, Dave Enos, Ken Frederick, Greg Highlands, Ken Reuwer, Bill Klein, Tom Neer, Ray Mack, Bob Hartley, Russ Palerea, Tim James, Greg Golden, Jeff Sieber, Mike Marks, Bill Lietzau, Whit Cobb, Jeff Norwitz, Mark Jacobson, Bill Monahan, John Ligouri, John McGuire, and many others assisted in reconstructing meetings to provide the most accurate accounting of events possible. They should all be proud to have served with honor during a critical time in our nation's history.

I am particularly humbled to call Alberto Mora a friend. His patriotism and genuine concern for American values and human rights is inspirational. Alberto restored my faith in political appointees, and I'm grateful for his guidance and the valor he so consistently demonstrates.

I am grateful as well for the support from Human Rights First. Elisa Massimino and the amazing staff there believe in American ideals and universal values. Raha Wala first told me they needed my voice. He, Scott Cooper, Brenda Bowser Soder, Corrine Duffy, Adam Jacobson, Heather Brandon, and others have worked tirelessly to illuminate the darkness of torture. Add in Sarah Dougherty of Physicians for Human Rights, Laura Pitter from Human Rights Watch, and Katherine Hawkins and Scott Roehm of the Constitution Project, and I've been blessed many times over.

I'm thankful for the support and assistance from a group known as the Dissident Psychologists, including Stephen Soldz, Steven Reisner, Nathaniel Raymond, and Jeffrey Kaye, as well as Heather O'Beirne Kelly from the APA, for ensuring I had access to documents and the various perspectives surrounding the issues of psychologist involvement in national security interrogations.

I also want to express my gratitude to the ACLU for obtaining so many e-mails and correspondence the US government had denied me access to, and to Robert Fein, who tracked those e-mails down and sent me so much correspondence regarding these issues over the years. The ACLU and Knights First Amendment Institute were instrumental in challenging censorship and protecting the First Amendment. I'm especially grateful for the support from the ACLU's Brett Max Kaufman and Knight Columbia's Alex Abdo. In the same vein, special thanks go to the researchers who provided me with material, support, and encouragement, including Par Anders Granhag, Aldert Vrij, Sharon Leal, Zarah Verhnam, Shane O'Mara, Melissa Russano, Maria Hartwig, John Horgan, Mia Bloom, and Chris Meissner.

Senators John McCain and Dianne Feinstein both urged me to continue to speak out against torture, and Senator Carl Levin paved the way by first illuminating the darkness and insisting my story be known. The courage and patriotism of these and others within the Congress who have worked so diligently to set the record straight on our shameful national policy decision to use torture as an instrument of national power cannot be overstated. So many in the media also carried that torch, long before it became popular to do so.

I also want to thank all of those friends and colleagues, far too many to list, who encouraged me to write this book and supported me during this process. Without that support network, this book would not have been possible.

Finally, this book is dedicated to my wife, Joanne, and family, who to this day know little about so much that I was involved in. Joanne's father and my father were partners on the Harrison, New Jersey, Police Department Detective Bureau. I joined their law enforcement ranks in 1979 when I stood in the US District Courthouse in Newark, New Jersey, as the chief deputy US marshal administered my first oath of office: "I pledge to protect and defend the Constitution of the United States, from all enemies, both foreign and domestic."

To me, those were more than just words. It was a conscious decision on my part that I might have to lay down my life for my country; and in fact I have given much of my life to my country. The pieces that were left went to Joanne, Matt, and Megan. They missed out on much of my life, just as I missed out on so much of theirs. When you are gone for extended periods, working undercover, when you run out in the middle of the night to respond to a call, when you have to worry every time the phone rings in the middle of the night or when someone knocks at the door, dreading that it might be that notification that any law enforcement officer's spouse dreads, life is not entirely normal, on either side of the family equation.

My wife recently heard me on the phone recounting some of the issues in this book and said: "Who are you? I don't really know you!" A revealing comment from the woman who has been married to me for more than thirty-five years.

My world was filled with murderers, rapists, child abusers, and terrorists, the worst in society. I tried never to bring the job home and expose my family to those things that had become routine to me, so I compartmentalized my work life from my home life, and my job was the priority. There was a point in my career when that changed, and my wife remembers the call when I said, "Enough is enough. From now on the family will come first," but a lot of water had flowed under the bridge before I got to that point.

Much of what I wrote in this book my family will be learning about for the first time. I hope it gives them some comfort to read about what I intentionally hid from them for so many years. Britt Mallow would tell everyone on the CITF that their grandchildren would ask what they did during the war on terror. I want my precious granddaughter, Candace Jade, who was born into a world of incredible advantages and disadvantages, to know I did my job.

GLOSSARY OF ABBREVIATIONS

BSCT   Behavioral Science Consultation Team, pronounced "biscuit," an integrated approach to interrogations.

CENTCOM   Central Command. Based at MacDill AFB in Tampa, CENTCOM has military responsibility for a broad swath of the Middle East and Muslim world, generally.

CIA   Central Intelligence Agency.

CID   Army Criminal Investigation Command.

CITF   Criminal Investigation Task Force, the group I led at Gitmo. Our assignment was to produce RTBs (reasons to believe) for the president and to assemble evidence in preparing detainees for trial before a military tribunal. We also were responsible for assessing the potential risks associated with the transfer or release of detainees from Gitmo.

CJTF   Combined Joint Task Force.

DIA   Defense Intelligence Agency.

DITMAC   Department of Defense Insider Threat Management and Analysis Center.

DOD   Department of Defense.

DOJ   Department of Justice.

DOS   Department of State.

EIT   Enhanced interrogation techniques, including sleep deprivation, waterboarding, etc.

EO   Executive Order, issued by the president.

FBI   Federal Bureau of Investigation.

FM 34-52   Army Field Manual on Intelligence Interrogation

GTMO   US Naval Base at Guantanamo Bay, Cuba, pronounced "Gitmo."

GWOT   Global War on Terror.

HIG   High-Value Detainee Interrogation Group.

HUMINT   Human Intelligence.

ISG   Iraq Survey Group.

JAGC   Judge Advocate General's Corps.

JCS   Joint Chiefs of Staff.

JPRA   Joint Personnel Recovery Agency.

JTF   Joint task force. Two JTFs play a central role in this book: JTF-160, which was responsible for detention facilities at GTMO, and JTF-170, which was handed primary responsibility for interrogations. JTF-GTMO was established to combine the functions of JTF-160 and JTF-170.

KSM   Khalid Sheikh Mohammed.

LEA   Law enforcement agency.

NCIS   Naval Criminal Investigative Service, the group from which I was detailed to CTIF. NCIS serves as the Department of the Navy's FBI and CIA.

NSA   National Security Agency.

OGA   Other Government Agency, the required way of referring to the CIA in all matters involving detainees.

OGC   Office of General Counsel.

OLC   Office of Legal Counsel.

OSI   Office of Special Investigations.

RDI   Rendition, Detention and Interrogation, the broad name for the CIA's prisoner- and intel-gathering operation. Maintained "black sites" in multiple foreign locations.

RTB   Reason to Believe, the legal requirement imposed on the president to move detainees to military trial. Our job was to provide the president with RTB evidence.

SASC   Senate Armed Services Committee.

SCIF   Sensitive Compartmented Information Facility; spaces immune from electronic snooping and other unauthorized disclosures.

SERE   Survive, Evade, Resist and Escape. Originally developed to train military personnel at risk of being captured by the enemy, the program was later applied to enhanced interrogation techniques patterned after those American POWs had faced in previous wars—hence, SERE-EITs.

SIGINT   Signals Intelligence.

SMU   Special Missions Unit.

SOCOM   Special Operations Command.

SOLIC   Special Operations and Low-Intensity Conflict.

SOUTHCOM   Southern Command, also based at MacDill AFB, oversees military special-operations forces. SOUTHCOM includes Navy SEALS, Army Green Berets, and other forward-operating and covert units.

SSCI   Senate Select Committee on Intelligence.

UCMJ   Uniform Code of Military Justice.

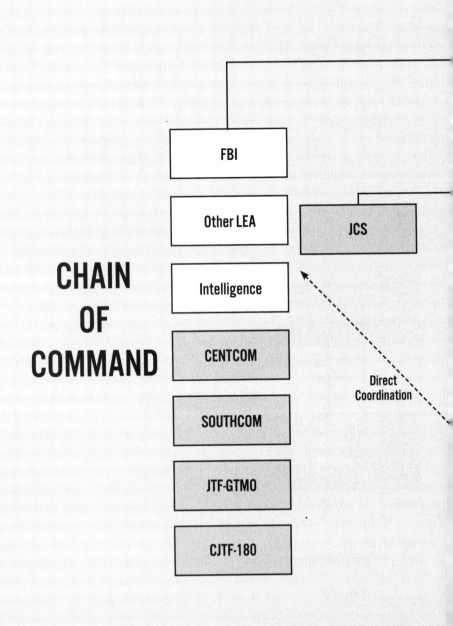

CHAIN
OF
COMMAND

FBI

Other LEA

JCS

Intelligence

CENTCOM

SOUTHCOM

JTF-GTMO

CJTF-180

Direct
Coordination

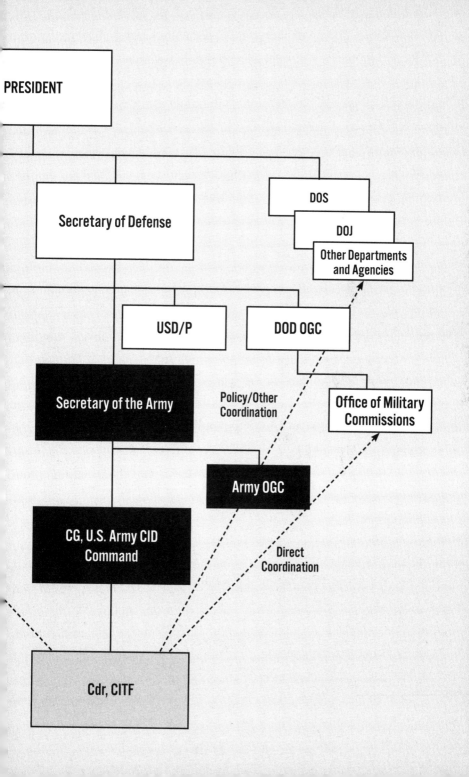

PRESIDENT

Secretary of Defense

DOS

DOJ

Other Departments and Agencies

USD/P

DOD OGC

Secretary of the Army

Policy/Other Coordination

Office of Military Commissions

Army OGC

CG, U.S. Army CID Command

Direct Coordination

Cdr, CITF